Christmas, 2006

Dear Rebecca,

    Another special book for my very special friend.

    Merry Christmas!

Love,
Marlene

Welcome

YOU CAN almost taste the fresh-baked gingerbread cookies, smell the fragrant pine boughs of the Christmas tree and feel the warmth of a crackling fire when you page through this newest edition of the annual Christmas book for country women.

Country Woman Christmas 2006 is packed from cover to cover with the kind of festive and fun holiday ideas you want to make this special season your family's best ever. Three big sections—"Christmas Decorating," "Holiday Recipes" and "Seasonal Crafts"—are brimming with new, never-before-published home decor, delectable foods and clever handcrafts sure to delight you and your loved ones for years to come.

You'll also find inspirational true stories of Christmas miracles...yummy bonus recipes in our special "World Cookie Exchange" section...artistic secrets from talented Christmas designers...and much, much more.

So settle back with a cup of hot cocoa, play some holiday music and let *Country Woman Christmas 2006* help you make this magical season your most memorable.

Contents

48

72

112

Pictured on front cover:
Gingerbread Christmas Cottage (p. 18)

4

Holiday Rush

Snowflakes falling from the sky
Crowning shoppers filing by
Blinking lights and lots of noise
Busy little girls and boys

Lots of trinkets, lots of treasures
Merchandise beyond our measures
Hustle, bustle, hurry, quick
It's almost time to see St. Nick

Moms and dads and children, too
Buying special gifts brand new
Homeward bound with gifts and toys
And thoughts of happy Christmas joys.

—*Gwen Baxter, Eckville, Alberta*

Editor
Michelle Bretl

Art Directors
Kathy Crawford, Lori Arndt

Executive Editor/Books
Heidi Reuter Lloyd

Senior Editor/Books
Mark Hagen

Craft Editor
Jane Craig

Proofreader
Linne Bruskewitz

Layout Designer
Emma Acevedo

Associate Layout Designer
Catherine Fletcher

Contributing Editor
Kathleen Anderson

Contributing Copy Editor
Kris Krueger

Editorial Assistant
Barb Czysz

Food Editor
Janaan Cunningham

Assistant Food Editor
Karen Scales

Contributing Home Economist
Mary Beth Jung

Senior Recipe Editor
Sue A. Jurack

Recipe Editor
Mary King

Contributing Recipe Editor
Susan Guenther

Test Kitchen Assistant
Rita Krajcir

Studio Photographers
Rob Hagen, Dan Roberts,
Jim Wieland

Associate Studio Photographer
Lori Foy

Food Stylists
Sarah Thompson, Joylyn Trickel

Contributing Food Stylists
Suzanne Breckenridge,
Sue Draheim, Mary Franz,
Lorene Frohling, Julie Herzfeldt,
Jennifer Janz, Jim Rude

Set Stylists
Sue Myers, Jennifer Bradley Vent

Contributing Set Stylists
Julie Ferron, Stephanie Marchese

Associate Set Stylist
Melissa Haberman

Photo Studio Coordinator
Suzanne Kern

Creative Director
Ardyth Cope

**Senior Vice President,
 Editor in Chief**
Catherine Cassidy

President
Barbara Newton

Founder
Roy Reiman

©2006 Reiman Media Group, Inc.
5400 S. 60th Street
Greendale WI 53129

International Standard Book Number: 0-89821-506-4
International Standard Serial Number: 1093-6750

Christmas Decorating

Creative Candles

...Will Make Your Season Bright

THE GLOW of flickering wicks...the eye-catching colors of wax...the sensational scents...candles cast an irresistible spell of golden warmth that radiates through an entire room. It's no wonder they're such popular decorations for the Christmas season.

Still, many of the decorated holiday candles sold in stores can be pricey. So what if you don't have money to burn? It's simple—just turn to the easy ideas here!

Country Woman Craft Editor Jane Craig has created six unique candle decorations using ordinary pillars, tapers and tea lights available at discount stores nearly everywhere. With a few basic craft supplies and household items, you can re-create these delightful designs in a flash.

Have some leftover bits of ribbon, a scrap of festive gift wrap or a glue gun? How about an extra Christmas garland, some natural evergreen boughs or a piece of decorative paper? If so, you're already well on your way toward creating gorgeous candle decor that'll have your friends and family asking, "Where did you find that?"

Before purchasing brand-new candles for these projects, check for any partially burnt candles you may already have on hand. Many of the candles used for these designs were previously burned...all it took was a merry "makeover" to give them a fresh and festive look.

So enjoy the creative project at right—a resplendent red trio of pillar candles draped with dewdrop-like strands—and check out the handy candle-burning hints listed below. Then turn the page to discover even more bright ideas!

Drizzled Delights
The secret to this dewy candle design is simple—a glue gun! Working with one candle at a time, hold the candle horizontally above a waxed paper-covered surface. Hold the glue gun 6 inches above the candle and apply glue strings randomly to the sides of the candle. Trim any excess glue from the bottom edge so the candle will stand up straight.

Candle-Burning Tips

- Keep the wick trimmed to 1/4 inch from the top of the candle.

- Light and then immediately extinguish candles when using them for the first time. They will light easier and burn more evenly when lit the second time.

- To extend the life of decorated pillar candles, place a tea light in the hollow of the candle and burn the tea light instead.

- Space taper candles at least 2 inches apart to prevent side wall burnout.

- Keep wick trimmings, matches and foreign objects out of the candle wax.

- Use a candle snuffer to put out candles to avoid spattering hot wax.

- Store candles in a cold, dry, dark place. Candles will fade if left in strong light for an extended period of time.

- Store tapers flat to prevent warping.

- Wrap stored candles in waxed paper to prevent color transfer and sticking.

Sparkling Water

To set this festive arrangement afloat, place three tall, narrow glass vases inside a footed glass bowl. (Place floral adhesive on the bottom of the vases if needed to secure them in place.) Partially fill the vases with water and place a tea light inside each. Form a purchased seasonal garland into a circle and arrange it on the bowl around the vases.

Gift-Wrapped Glow

Put your scraps of Christmas wrapping paper to good use! Just cut an appropriate-size design or motif from the paper, apply thinned white (tacky) glue or decoupage medium to the cutout and adhere it to the side of a pillar candle. If you like, glue on beads or outline the cutout with dimensional fabric/craft paint. Then let the candle dry.

Brilliant Bouquet

You can "grow" this showy decoration in just about any shallow (low-sided) vase that's long and narrow. Fill the vase with wet floral foam, then add natural pine greens and flowers, concealing the foam and vase. Spray the arrangement with artificial snow and let it dry. Stand taper candles in the center of the arrangement.

Ribbon Radiance

It's a cinch to lace up this lovely Christmas look. Simply wrap a piece of wide, open-weave ribbon around a pillar candle, leaving a gap between the ends of the ribbon. Starting at the bottom of the candle, lace the wide ribbon ends together using a piece of coordinating narrow satin ribbon. Tie the ends of the satin ribbon in a bow to secure it.

Shimmering Shade

This pretty paper creation is illuminated with a battery-operated candle. First, cut a piece of translucent paper to fit around a clear glass vase. Secure the paper to the vase using double-stick tape. Then put a battery-operated or wax candle in the vase and set it on a footed stand. Arrange artificial leaves, pinecones and Christmas ornaments around the stand.

Miniature Theme Trees

HAVE YOU ever dreamed of decorating your family's Christmas tree in an exciting new way? Maybe you've thought of trimming it totally in silver…or in gorgeous Victorian style…or in a medley of musical motifs. Then, you inevitably spot a spectacular tree in a store during the holidays—and you think of yet another idea!

The problem is, you already own more ornaments than you need to decorate your annual holiday tree. And the expense of buying enough new ones to fill up a full-size evergreen isn't very appealing.

But you don't have to forego the fun of creative tree trimming. Simply scale things down a bit—and decorate a *miniature* tree.

While smaller in size, mini trees still provide enough room for you to build on a theme using a variety of ornaments. These petite evergreens also take up less space in your house, and the decorating possibilities are endless.

For example, you could combine small souvenirs (such as the "Stille Nacht" trim from Austria below) from your vacation onto a "Vacation Memories" tree. Or, if you love snowmen (such as the ornament at left), let your passion run wild and decorate a tree entirely with those frosty figures.

To get your creative juices flowing, check out the quick theme ideas listed below…and see our showcase of miniature theme trees starting on the next page.

Creative Theme Ideas

Winter Warmers Tree

Bundle up the branches with little knit mittens, socks, sweaters, etc. Add a "clothesline" of mini clothespins and top the tree with a hat.

Family Photo Tree

Create a "family tree" with picture frame ornaments that display generations of photos. If you like, fit in small heirlooms as well.

Birds 'n' Birdhouses Tree

Are you an avian enthusiast? Show it with a tree full of tiny artificial birds and mini birdhouses. Accent it with nests of speckled eggs.

Simply Santa Tree

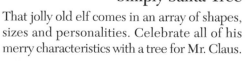

That jolly old elf comes in an array of shapes, sizes and personalities. Celebrate all of his merry characteristics with a tree for Mr. Claus.

Host of Angels Tree

What could be more divine than an evergreen of cheery cherubs? You could add angel hair and circles of thin gold garland for "halos."

Bells, Bells, Bells Tree

Ring in the season with beautiful bells of all kinds. If you like, make small photocopies of the song "Jingle Bells" and fit in those, too.

Child's Delight Tree

Make eyes light up with little toys such as dolls, trains, rocking horses and teddy bears. Wrap up tiny boxes to create gifts.

Completely Crimson Tree

What a striking idea—a pine trimmed totally in resplendent red. Or, focus on silver, gold, blue, white or any color you prefer.

Natural Wonders Tree

A FEELING of quiet serenity comes from a Christmas tree decorated with objects of nature. On the *au natural* evergreen shown here, dramatic peacock feathers are set off by more understated trims—artificial leaves and bunches of grapes, pinecones and small grapevine wreaths wrapped with embroidery floss in coordinating colors.

More "Natural Wonders" Ornament Options: Artificial poinsettias, berry sprigs, fruits (such as pears and oranges), walnuts or other nuts, snowflake ornaments or artificial snow, icicle ornaments, raffia bows, twigs glued in shapes (such as stars and hexagons), wheat stalks, dried flowers, eucalyptus.

Nutcracker Ballet Tree

REFLECTED on a miniature tree, the grace and romance of *The Nutcracker Ballet* can beautify your home all season long. Tutu-like pink tulle surrounds and tops the pretty pine shown here. Ballet slipper, bow and nutcracker ornaments are focal points, accented by small gold bead ornaments and frosted ball-shaped "sugarplums" in different colors.

More "Nutcracker Ballet" Ornament Options: Satin ribbon bows, velvet bows, tiny Christmas gift boxes, ballerinas, fairies, Christmas mice, snowflake ornaments or artificial snow, brass buttons, candy ornaments (such as chocolates, candy canes and bonbons), artificial gemstones, flowers, miniature dolls.

Christmas Kitchen Tree

SUGAR, spice and everything nice make this theme an extra sweet one for your country kitchen. On the tasteful tree shown here, miniature kitchen utensil, dish and dessert ornaments combine for a "yummy" Yuletide look. It's all wrapped up with Christmasy cookie cutters and a garland of red gingham ribbon.

More "Christmas Kitchen" Ornament Options: Bundles of cinnamon sticks, small spice containers or bags, measuring spoons and cups, real gingerbread cutout cookies, wooden spoons, a string of red berries or gumdrops, miniature foil muffin cups, pastry tips, cookie press disks.

A Merry Mix of Old World and New

By Heidi Lloyd of Burlington, Wisconsin

"FRÖHLICHE WEIHNACHTEN." That German phrase, meaning "Merry Christmas," seems just as appropriate in my home during the holiday season as the same words in English do.

That's because my Christmas decor blends the heritage of my father's family in Germany with the typical American traditions my mother's family follows. You might describe this seasonal style as "Old World Meets Small-Town Wisconsin," and it perfectly suits me, my husband, Mike, and our 11-year-old son, Paul.

My father came to the United States from West Germany as a foreign exchange student. As a young boy, he experienced the hardships of World War II and had even helped his mother and sisters jump from moving trains to escape bombs falling overhead. He dreamed of the land called "America," full of possibilities and opportunities.

After Dad attended high school for a year in Wisconsin, he went back to Germany but vowed to return and become a U.S. citizen. He did so several years later, the only member of his family to emigrate to the United States.

Now, whenever I visit my aunts, uncles and cousins still in Germany, I bring back souvenirs I can incorporate into our home decor. It's my way of bridging the gap between the old

THE DINING TABLE (at far left above) draws Heidi's family and friends with the warmth of candles, beautiful place settings and bright linens. The striking red cloth napkins reflect Heidi's penchant for buying linens as souvenirs of the special places she's visited. Purchased while she was in Berlin, Germany with her sister, Lisa, each napkin features an embroidered tree.

A BLAZING FIREPLACE (above) is made even more appealing with gorgeous seasonal decor, starting with elegant Christmas stockings for everyone in the family. A large Father Christmas figure brings his own glow to the living room with a lit lantern. On the mantel, wooden nutcrackers and other unique treasures from Heidi's trips to Germany make charming conversation pieces.

"O TANNENBAUM" truly sums up Heidi's large Christmas tree (at right), which sparkles with hand-blown glass ornaments from Germany and elsewhere. Her favorites include old-time Father Christmas figures, angels, snowmen and unusual shapes such as birds and pears. Even the garland is a string of tiny glass ornaments.

A CHRISTMASY KITCHEN (above) is a must in Heidi's house during December. Next to that room, a second dining area (at left) sparkles with more Christmas trees, candles and plenty of goodies for guests.

world and new…and it makes me feel closer to Dad, who is now gone, and his family overseas.

Shopping in Germany at Christmastime is especially enjoyable. During the holiday season, cities all across the country have Christkindl markets—open-air markets with booths that sell ornaments, toys, linens, sausages, stollens, nativity scenes, crafts, cookies, flowers, hot spiced wine…you name it. It's like a farmer's market, a flea market and your favorite Christmas shop all rolled into one!

My passion, though, is hand-blown glass ornaments. Many in my collection were purchased in Germany, and I now have enough of those decorations to fill the entire 7-foot Christmas tree in our living room…although it's taken me 20 years to accumulate them all!

I especially love my glass ornaments that are shaped like old-time Father Christmases (each just a little different than the others), angels (who all look so regal, in different ways), snowmen and unusual designs such as birds and pears.

My non-glass ornaments go on the three—or more—other Christmas trees I put up, each of which has a theme. Most recently, I decorated a slim tree with 2- to 3-inch-tall angels, all from Germany and featuring shiny fabric dresses and translucent wings. I also had fun creating a small nutcracker tree, trimmed completely with those traditional figures.

In fact—to me—nutcrackers "say" Christmas the most. I've collected dozens over the years and display them in just about every nook and cranny during the holidays—the mantel of the living room fireplace, on top of the entertainment center, above the kitchen cabinets and on tables. Their bright colors and classic, timeless look add to the festive atmosphere of the house. I even have nutcrackers that resemble snowmen and teddy bears…there's quite a variety!

Still, like many of the other Christmas decorations in our home, my nutcrackers all have one thing in common—they bring back special memories of a far-off country and warm my heart with thoughts of family all season long. 🕊

THE DELIGHTFUL DETAILS of the hand-blown glass ornaments on Heidi's Christmas tree (above left) invite a closer look. On the nearby coffee table, a traditional German pyramid (above) depicts a Christmas market scene surrounded by candles and has propeller-like blades that rotate when the candles burn. Looking down at all of these festive decorations, wood nutcracker kings, soldiers and other characters stand on the entertainment center (below). Each Christmas season, Heidi displays dozens of the German-style nutcrackers.

Make Your Own...

Home Sweet Home

for the Holidays!

YOU CAN just imagine the cozy Christmas scene that would be found inside this colorful cookie house: a crackling fire in the hearth...children by the Christmas tree...Mom baking a batch of gingerbread...Dad reading aloud "'Twas the night before Christmas..."

From the candy cobblestone path and icing evergreens to the gumdrop roof and peppermint posts, this jolly gingerbread cottage from Blanche Comiskey of Franklin, Wisconsin draws you into an enchanting Christmas wonderland.

Want to delight your family and friends with this merry holiday house? It's easy! Simply follow the step-by-step directions we've included here.

Below, you'll find a complete list of the ingredients you'll need for the delicious gingerbread and sweet decorations. Plus, we've included all of the necessary patterns and even how-to photos to help you with the assembly.

Except for the cotton smoke and lollipop sticks, this eye-catching creation is completely edible...but you may decide it's too beautiful to eat!

Gingerbread Christmas Cottage

DOUGH:
    1 cup shortening
    1/2 cup boiling water
    1 cup packed dark brown sugar
    1 cup dark molasses
    6 cups all-purpose flour
    2 teaspoons salt
    2 teaspoons baking soda
    1 teaspoon ground ginger
    1 teaspoon ground nutmeg
    1/4 teaspoon ground cloves
Patterns on page 21
ICING AND ASSEMBLY:
    16 cups confectioners' sugar, *divided*
    12 tablespoons meringue powder, *divided*
    2 teaspoons cream of tartar, *divided*
    1-1/2 cups warm water, *divided*
    14 red spice gumdrops
    8 large candy canes (6 inches), *divided*
    Multicolored nonpareils
    1 red-hot candy
    18 leaf-shaped spearmint gumdrops, *divided*
About 150 multicolored spice gumdrops, halved vertically
Edible glitter
    10 ice cream sugar cones
Green paste food coloring
    30 chocolate rock candies
    21 pieces candy corn in Christmas colors *or* green gumdrops
    8 miniature candy canes (about 2-1/4 inches)
    10 green spice gumdrops
    4 green rock candy suckers
    1 large cotton ball
Pastry tips—star tips #16 and #20, round tips #3 and #7, and leaf tip #67
Pastry bags

Foam core board (20 inches x 16 inches x 1/2 inch)
Small cans for propping

In a large mixing bowl, combine shortening and water. Add brown sugar and molasses; mix well. Combine flour, salt, baking soda and spices; beat into molasses mixture until blended. Divide into three portions; chill overnight.

Trace the full patterns onto waxed paper; cut out. Trace the remaining (halved) patterns onto waxed paper as directed on the patterns; cut out.

With a lightly floured rolling pin, roll one portion of dough to 1/8-inch thickness directly onto a lightly greased and floured baking sheet. With a sharp knife, cut out two front/back house pieces. On one front/back house piece, score window and door.

Roll out second portion of dough. Cut out two 8-1/2-in. x 6-in. rectangles for roof.

Roll out third portion of dough. Position house side pattern on dough; cut out two pieces. On each piece, score two windows. Cut out one 2-3/8-inch x 1-3/8-inch rectangle for left side of chimney and a 1-3/8-inch x 7/8-inch rectangle for right side of chimney. Roll out scraps to cut out patterns for sides of chimney; sides and roof of porch; and front, sides and roofs of dormers. Score dormer windows.

Bake at 375° for 8-10 minutes or until lightly browned. Cool for 2 minutes; place patterns over baked dough and trim. Cut out door and windows completely. (Set aside door cutout; discard window cutouts.) Cool on wire racks.

To make icing: Prepare only one batch of icing at a time. For each batch, in a large mixing bowl, combine 4 cups confectioners' sugar, 3 tablespoons meringue powder, 1/2 teaspoon cream of tartar and 6 tablespoons water. Beat on low speed for 5-10 minutes or until stiff peaks form. Place a damp cloth over bowl and cover tightly between uses.

To assemble frame of house: Place front and sides of house and fronts of dormers on a waxed paper-lined flat surface. Cut a small hole in a corner of a pastry bag; insert star tip #16. Fill two-thirds full with icing. Pipe curtains in the house and dormer windows. Outline frames of windows and doorway with round tip #3.

For shutters, roll out 10 red gumdrops to 1/16-inch thickness; cut each into a 1-1/8-inch x 3/8-inch rectangle. Roll out four red gumdrops for dormer shutters; cut each into a 7/8-inch x 1/4-inch rectangle. Attach house and dormer shutters with a dab of icing on each side of windows.

Using tip #16, pipe decorative trim on the front and back rooflines and peaks of the house, taking care to avoid the edges. Let dry completely.

Pipe icing along base and one side of front wall and the adjoining side wall. Place at right angles to each other on foam core board so front of house is 6-1/4-in. from one narrow side of board; prop with small cans. Pipe icing along inside and outside edges for added stability. Repeat with second side section and back. Let dry completely.

Cut 3-1/2-inch pieces from the straight end of four large candy canes (set aside curved ends for another use). Pipe icing along each outside corner of house with star tip #20;

(continued on next page)

press straight candy cane pieces into each corner. Let dry completely, about 4 hours.

For dormers: Insert tip #16 into pastry bag; fill two-thirds full with icing. Pipe icing along one side of front of dormer and one adjoining side wall. Position at right angles to each other and place on waxed paper; pipe icing along inside edge for added stability. Hold in place until secure. Repeat with second side. Repeat for second dormer. Let dry completely with front side up.

To assemble roof: Generously pipe icing along top edges of house. Position roof pieces so there is a 5/8-inch overhang in front and back. Pipe icing along the joining edges. Prop bottom of roof pieces with cans until roof is completely dry.

On right roof piece, position one dormer 1-1/2 inches from left side, 1-1/2 inches up from the bottom and above the lower window, aligning so dormer front is perpendicular to board. Pipe dots of icing to mark the position of bottom dormer corners. Pipe icing onto back edges of dormer; attach to roof. Hold in place until secure, about 1 minute. Repeat with sec-

Assembling Dormers

Fig. 1: Pipe icing along one side of the front of the dormer and one adjoining side wall. Position at right angles to each other and place on waxed paper; pipe icing along inside edge for added stability. Hold in place until secure. Repeat with second side. Repeat for second dormer. Let dry completely with front side up.

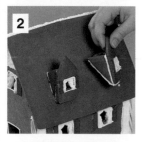

Fig. 2: On right roof piece, position one dormer 1-1/2 inches from left side, 1-1/2 inches up from the bottom and above the lower window, aligning so dormer front is perpendicular to board. Pipe dots of icing to mark the position of the bottom dormer corners. Pipe icing onto back edges of dormer; attach to roof.

Fig. 3: Attach dormer roofs with icing so there is a 1/4-inch overhang in front of dormer.

Fig. 4: Pipe icing along top edge of the dormer roofs; press 2-inch straight candy cane pieces into each. Let dry completely.

ond dormer. Let dry completely.

Attach dormer roofs with icing so there is a 1/4-inch overhang in front. Cut two 2-inch straight pieces from candy canes. Pipe icing along top edge of dormer roofs; press straight candy cane pieces into each. Let dry completely.

For chimney and door: Spread chimney pieces and door with icing; dip into multicolored nonpareils. With tip #3, pipe a dot of icing on door and attach red-hot for the handle. Let dry. Pipe icing along left edge and bottom of door; position door so it is ajar.

Using tip #16 and icing, attach chimney pieces to plain side of roof, positioning the back chimney piece 1-1/2 inches from back edge of roof and working clockwise with remaining pieces. Pipe icing around top of chimney and along chimney seams. Cut one 5-inch piece and one 1-1/4-inch piece from the straight ends of two candy canes. Pipe icing along top edge between roof pieces; press straight pieces into icing.

For porch: Place porch roof smooth side down on a work surface. To attach sides, pipe icing along the long side of each triangle and position against porch roof. Invert to dry.

For porch support posts, cut two 2-3/4-inch straight pieces from candy canes. Insert each into a leaf-shaped spearmint gumdrop; position 1 in. from house and 3 inches apart on each side of doorway. Secure gumdrops with icing. Let dry. Attach porch roof to posts and house with icing; prop with small cans and let dry.

To decorate roof: With tip #20, pipe two rows of icing along bottom of chimney side of roof. Press five halved gumdrops of different colors into icing in a row; repeat until one horizontal row is finished. Begin the second row with the second color from row one. Repeat nine times, slightly overlapping each row until one roof piece is covered with a diagonally patterned design.

On dormer side of roof and starting at bottom edge, repeat procedure for gumdrop shingles. Attach gumdrops to the dormer and porch roofs in the same pattern as roof of house. Pipe icing onto sides of porch roof. Let dry.

For finishing touches: Using round tip #7, pipe icing icicles. Sprinkle with edible glitter.

To make trees, use a serrated knife to carefully score and cut ice cream cones to desired heights. Tint a portion of icing with green food coloring. Using leaf tip #67 and beginning at bottom of ice cream cones, pipe icing in rows; sprinkle with edible glitter. Place on waxed paper to harden. Using tip #7, pipe snow on the trees and sprinkle with edible glitter. Set aside.

For path, using tip #20 and beginning at the door, pipe icing in a zigzag pattern. Press chocolate rock candies 1/8 inch apart onto pathway. Position candy corn, point side up, along both sides of path. Working in small sections, frost the base board with icing for snow and sprinkle with edible glitter.

For each corner fence, use tip #7 and white icing to attach two miniature candy canes to board. Arrange trees on base along with green gumdrops, rock candy suckers and remaining leaf-shaped gumdrops for bushes; secure with icing. For smoke, pull and stretch the cotton ball; attach with icing to inside of chimney. **Yield:** 1 gingerbread house. 🎄

GINGERBREAD CHRISTMAS COTTAGE PATTERNS
(See instructions for dimensions of house roof and remaining chimney pieces.)

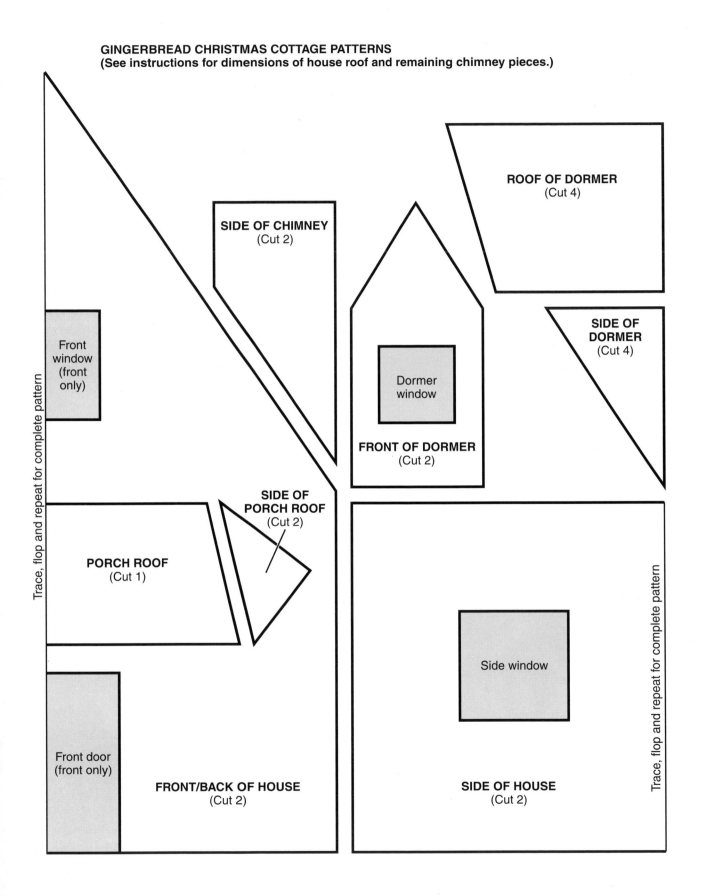

Trace, flop and repeat for complete pattern

Front window (front only)

SIDE OF CHIMNEY
(Cut 2)

ROOF OF DORMER
(Cut 4)

SIDE OF DORMER
(Cut 4)

Dormer window

FRONT OF DORMER
(Cut 2)

SIDE OF PORCH ROOF
(Cut 2)

PORCH ROOF
(Cut 1)

Side window

Trace, flop and repeat for complete pattern

Front door (front only)

FRONT/BACK OF HOUSE
(Cut 2)

SIDE OF HOUSE
(Cut 2)

Christmas Miracles

Chance encounters…unexpected blessings…lucky coincidences… read about these unforgettable Christmas events in the lives of country women.

The Divine Doll

WHEN my husband's company started downsizing and he lost ▮▮▮, money was extremely tight. It was difficult to tell our 7-year-old daughter that she wouldn't be getting the doll she wanted for Christmas. I prayed about it, hoping for a miracle.

A week before Christmas, we were walking in a department store parking lot. I happened to glance at something on the ground. It was a $5 bill! We decided to go in the store to check the price of the doll, but our elation quickly turned to disappointment when we saw the price was still out of reach.

My husband and I didn't notice the nearby mark-down table, but our daughter did. "Look, Mom and Dad," she called out. "Here's the doll I want!"

I was amazed. It was the same doll, only without the box and with a small smudge on the dress. I looked at the price. It was 75% off—making the final price about $5.

When we went to pay for the doll, the salesclerk said, "Oh, this came from the mark-down table."

"Actually," I said, "it came from Heaven."
~Margaret Cagle, Jacksonville, Florida

Lost and Found

ON A SNOWY Christmas Eve, my husband and I left my mother's home, where we were staying, to attend church 40 miles away. Afterward, I wanted to stop at the nearby cemetery to visit my grandparents' graves. My grandpa had only recently passed away.

In the dark with snow whipping around us, my husband pulled the car up to the unlit cemetery. He stayed in the running car, leaving the headlights beaming in what we thought was the right direction.

As I trudged through the snow in my high heels and peered around, I quickly grew frustrated. I couldn't remember exactly where my grandparents were buried. It was so dark, and everything was covered with snow! The flat headstones were completely hidden. I couldn't even be sure I was in the right section of the cemetery.

Feeling hopeless and upset, I was about to give up. Finally, I called out in desperation, "Grandpa, Grandma, where are you? I came to wish you a merry Christmas, but I can't find you!"

On impulse, I suddenly stopped walking and knelt at the stone directly beneath me. I brushed away the heavy snow…only to see my grandpa's name right at my feet!

Tears rolled down my cheeks. I cleared off the markers…and wished my grandparents a merry Christmas.

~Kim Villalva, Lawton, Oklahoma

❦ In the Nick of Time

OUR DAUGHTER desperately wanted just one thing for Christmas—a cupboard she could play "house" with. We couldn't afford much, but I ordered a small cardboard cupboard through a department store catalog about a month before December 25.

On Christmas Eve, to my dismay, the cupboard still had not arrived. By the time the last mail delivery came, it was too late to find an open store. I had absolutely no idea how "Santa" was going to come up with a cupboard.

At church that evening, I prayed for a miracle. I told my friend the situation as we were leaving. She said, "Why, my mother's neighbor makes children's cupboards and sells them…I wonder if he has any left?"

I couldn't wait to get home and call this man. But by then, it was nearly 10:00. I was afraid he wouldn't even answer the phone. Lo and behold, he did answer— and said he had only one cupboard left. My husband would have to drive to another town to get it.

By the time my husband got home and we got "ready" for Santa's visit, it was early Christmas morning. We'd only just fallen asleep when our daughter came creeping into our bedroom to announce that Santa had indeed brought the cupboard she'd wanted so much—and it even had wooden doors.

The department store cupboard never did come, but—miraculously—it didn't need to.

~Joyce Orshoski, Castalia, Ohio

❦ Sweet Tradition Saved

AFTER we lost our home and farm in a flood, we moved into a trailer nearby and stored what possessions we'd recovered in the empty house. Though our lives had changed drastically, I was determined to continue my annual tradition of making Christmas cookies with our grandchildren.

On the day of the event, I stirred up a double batch of dough and set out all the colored sugars and cookie cutters for the children. When they arrived, eager for the fun to start, I was dismayed to discover that something was missing—my rolling pin! I realized it must have been packed in a box and put somewhere in the old house.

Thinking there were no other options, I rushed over to the dark, cold, gutted house. Without a flashlight, I blindly stumbled my way over piles and piles of possessions, feeling around inside box after box. But the rolling pin was nowhere to be found.

I stood still for several minutes, on the verge of tears, thinking about my waiting grandchildren. Finally, I reached down one last time…and my fingers closed over a smooth, wooden shape. The rolling pin!

At that moment, I felt the presence of a guardian angel, who guided me to the right place.

~Connie Frieden, Taylor, Missouri

❦ The Kindness of Strangers

IT WAS Christmas Eve, and we'd been living in Canada for a few months. My husband had only recently found a job, and we'd sold just about everything we could to pay for the trip.

We had nothing of the usual holiday trappings—no Christmas tree, no turkey, not even a single gift for our three children. We'd resigned ourselves to the fact that our first Christmas in Canada was going to be an unhappy one.

Suddenly, there was a knock on the door. It was our neighbor, with whom we'd never spoken except to say "hi" when passing on the street.

"My wife and I would like you and the children to join us tomorrow for Christmas dinner," he said. I stood there, stunned. I couldn't believe it—these people were offering to open their home to strangers on Christmas Day.

When we went to their house, they not only served dinner, they also had a toy for each of our children and an ornament for us on the Christmas tree.

From that day on, we were best friends. These generous people are now gone, but we'll never forget them and our first Christmas in Canada.

~Maria Louis, Tillsonburg, Ontario

A Touch of Whimsy

This designer draws on ordinary items to create Christmas magic.

SNOWFLAKES, sugar cubes, kids' toys—it's the simple things that inspire Angela Evans. This Farmington, Minnesota artist finds delight in everyday items and uses them as the foundation for all kinds of Christmas designs.

"I love the holidays, so it isn't hard for me to develop new ideas," says Angela. "Even something as simple as seeing a new color is enough to inspire me to start creating.

"For example, I spotted a soft shade of blue that I really liked, especially when white snowflakes were silhouetted against it. I combined that hue with a cheery red and creamy white—and decided that these colors were the perfect palette for a snowman-based theme."

From there, Angela quickly got to work on the actual figures. "I wanted the snowman shape to be simple, reminiscent of the vintage snowmen I remember from my childhood," she shares.

"At the same time, I wanted to update him and give

him some fresh, fun accents like candy canes, buttoned shirts and clown-type hats."

The end result was a collection of smiling characters Angela named "Snowy Bright." She used a variety of materials to fashion the figures and trims, ranging from wool felt and glass to what she calls "paper pulp"—a papier mache-like material coated in

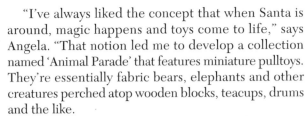

FROM PARADES of animal pull-toys lead by grand Santas to merry snowmen capped with clown hats, Angela Evans' playful creations for Christmas come in a wide variety of festive forms.

glass glitter. Some of the fabric versions sport numbered pockets and can be used as Advent calendars.

Driven by Design

"I don't have a favorite medium to work with," Angela says. "I draw out the idea first, then choose the material that seems to work best with the concept. I've crafted decorations from paper, tulle, velvet, paint and more and have also had designs cast in resin.

"I've even used food to create prototypes for a line of characters called 'Simply Scrumptious.' I started by thinking about sugar cubes and snowmen, then graduated to grabbing a bag of marshmallows, some frosting and other edible items and building snowmen in my kitchen."

While Frosty figures big in Angela's cache of decorations—he recently served as the model for a new flurry of characters wearing crimson top hats called "Merry Holidays"— the thought of Santa also stirs her imagination.

"I've always liked the concept that when Santa is around, magic happens and toys come to life," says Angela. "That notion led me to develop a collection named 'Animal Parade' that features miniature pulltoys. They're essentially fabric bears, elephants and other creatures perched atop wooden blocks, teacups, drums and the like.

"I also crafted a jolly St. Nick to lead the procession. The collection is fun to have 'marching' along a mantel or down the center of a dining table."

Family Affair

Art has always been a part of Angela's life. "My mother and grandmother did a lot of crafting, and I followed in their footsteps, trying everything from crocheting and quilting to sewing, beading and decorating cakes," she says. "I also studied art in college, and my two children—though they haven't been directly involved in my work—are a constant inspiration.

"Both of them are grown, but we still find time to create things together around the holidays. One of our favorite activities is decorating sugar cookies at Christmastime. The kids are really good at it, and we all try to outdo each other by coming up with the most unique way to decorate a cookie."

Travel has become another avenue for ideas. "It's my new passion," she enthuses. "I get to see artists and craftspeople from all over, and I love how each trip energizes my creativity.

"I plan to keep visiting new places and learning all I can, because there's an unlimited number of holiday ideas out there, just waiting for me to find them."

Editor's Note: Angela's designs are available at retail stores nationwide. For information on stores near you, contact Midwest/Seasons of Cannon Falls, 32057-64th Ave., Cannon Falls MN 55006, or check the company Web site, *www.seasonsofcannonfalls.com.* ▲

Holiday Recipes

Frothy Orange-Pineapple Cooler (p. 29)
Asparagus Pie
Spiced Sausage Patties (p. 28)

A Bountiful Brunch

★ Asparagus Pie

This hearty quiche is as attractive as it is flavorful! It looks complicated to make but is actually a simple recipe. The secret is the crust—it's refrigerated pizza dough that I season with basil and Parmesan cheese. But the asparagus spokes are what make this pie special for the holidays. It almost seems too nice to cut, but we're always glad we did when we taste a slice.

~Mary Lou Wayman, Salt Lake City, Utah

    1/4 pound fresh asparagus, trimmed
      2 teaspoons vegetable oil
    1/2 cup grated Parmesan cheese
      2 teaspoons dried basil
      1 package (13.8 ounces) refrigerated pizza crust
      3 bacon strips, diced
      1 medium onion, chopped
      5 eggs
    1/2 cup milk
    1/8 teaspoon salt
 Dash ground nutmeg
 1-1/2 cups (6 ounces) shredded Swiss cheese
      1 tablespoon all-purpose flour

1. In a large skillet, cook the asparagus in boiling water for 2 minutes; drain. Toss with oil; set aside.

2. Combine Parmesan cheese and basil; sprinkle half over work surface. Place pizza dough on surface; roll into a 12-in. circle. Sprinkle with remaining Parmesan mixture; gently press into dough with a rolling pin. Transfer to a greased 9-in. springform pan. Press dough onto the bottom and 1-1/2 in. up the sides of pan.

3. Line unpricked dough with a double thickness of heavy-duty foil. Bake at 425° for 8 minutes. Remove foil; bake 5 minutes longer. Place on a wire rack. Reduce heat to 350°.

4. In a small skillet, cook bacon over medium heat until crisp; using a slotted spoon, remove bacon to paper towels. Drain, reserving 1 tablespoon drippings. In the drippings, saute onion until tender; drain.

5. In a large bowl, whisk the eggs, milk, salt and nutmeg. Stir in bacon and onion. Toss the Swiss cheese and flour; stir into egg mixture. Pour into the crust. Arrange asparagus in a spoke-like pattern on top.

6. Place pan on a baking sheet. Bake for 35-40 minutes or until a knife inserted near the center comes out clean. Let stand for 10 minutes before removing sides of pan. Cut into wedges. **Yield:** 6 servings.

★ Fruit Compote

Whether you prepare this fruit dish for brunch, offer it as an appetizer or top it with a dollop of whipped cream for a light dessert, your guests will be happy. It's brimming with color and flavor and is especially welcome during wintertime.

~Dorothy Diehl Carnine, Angora, Nebraska

      1 can (20 ounces) unsweetened pineapple tidbits
      1 can (11 ounces) mandarin oranges
      2 tablespoons quick-cooking tapioca
    1/4 cup orange juice concentrate
 1-1/2 cups seedless red grapes, halved
      1 package (10 ounces) frozen unsweetened sliced peaches
 1-1/2 cups fresh *or* frozen raspberries
      1 medium firm banana, sliced

1. Drain pineapple and oranges, reserving juice; set fruit aside. In a large microwave-safe bowl, combine tapioca and reserved juices; let stand for 5 minutes. Microwave, uncovered, on high for 2-3 minutes or until clear and thickened, stirring several times. Stir in orange juice concentrate.

2. In a large bowl, combine the pineapple, oranges, grapes and peaches. Add tapioca mixture; toss to coat. Cover and refrigerate overnight. Just before serving, stir in the raspberries and banana. **Yield:** 12 servings.

Editor's Note: This recipe was tested in a 1,100-watt microwave.

Fruit Compote

Orange Pull-Apart Coffee Ring

4. Sprinkle with reserved sugar mixture and remaining almonds. Bake on lowest oven rack at 350° for 38-42 minutes or until golden brown (cover loosely with foil if browning too quickly). Cool for 10 minutes before removing from pan to a wire rack. **Yield:** 12 servings.

★ Spiced Sausage Patties

(Pictured on page 26)

You've never tasted sausage quite like this before! The secret to this special recipe from South Africa lies in the spices, which include coriander, cloves, allspice and nutmeg. I've been cooking for a while, and this is one of my favorite recipes.
~ Heather Madgwick, Garden City, Kansas

    2-1/2 pounds ground beef
      1/2 pound ground pork
    2-1/4 teaspoons salt
    1-1/2 teaspoons ground coriander
        1 to 1-1/2 teaspoons ground allspice
      3/4 teaspoon ground cloves
      3/4 teaspoon pepper
      1/2 teaspoon ground nutmeg
      1/4 cup cider vinegar

1. Crumble beef and pork into a large bowl. Combine the seasonings; sprinkle over meat. Add vinegar and mix well. Cover and refrigerate for 1 hour.

2. Shape meat mixture into 2-1/2-in. patties. In a large skillet, cook patties over medium heat for 4-5 minutes on each side or until no longer pink. **Yield:** 2-1/2 dozen.

Ginger Pancakes With Lemon Sauce

I first tried these spice-laced hotcakes at my niece's house, and they quickly became my favorite breakfast item. Spreading cream cheese on each one and then topping the pancakes with the thick lemony sauce yields a tasty treat that's different from typical breakfast fare. ~Helen Snow, Litchfield, Nebraska

        1 cup sugar
      1/2 cup butter, cubed
      1/4 cup water
        3 tablespoons lemon juice
        1 teaspoon grated lemon peel
        1 egg, lightly beaten
BATTER:
        2 cups biscuit/baking mix
        1 egg
    1-1/3 cups milk
      1/4 cup light molasses
    1-1/2 teaspoons ground ginger
        1 teaspoon ground cinnamon
      1/2 teaspoon ground cloves
        1 carton (4 ounces) spreadable cream cheese

1. For lemon sauce, in a small saucepan, combine the first five ingredients. Bring to a boil over medium heat, stirring constantly. Remove from the heat. Whisk a small amount of hot

★ Orange Pull-Apart Coffee Ring

This coffee ring is an old family recipe that's long been a hit with anyone who's tried it. The yeast bread is a great Sunday treat—or the perfect way to kick off your holiday celebration.
~Beverly Hansen, Sunny Hills, Florida

        2 packages (1/4 ounce *each*) active dry yeast
    1-1/4 cups warm milk (110° to 115°)
        7 tablespoons sugar
        4 egg yolks
      1/3 cup butter, melted
        1 teaspoon salt
        4 to 4-1/4 cups all-purpose flour
TOPPING:
      2/3 cup sugar
        4 teaspoons grated orange peel
        3 tablespoons butter, melted
      1/2 cup slivered almonds, *divided*

1. In a large mixing bowl, dissolve yeast in warm milk. Add the sugar, egg yolks, butter, salt and 2 cups flour; beat until smooth. Stir in enough remaining flour to form a soft dough (dough will be sticky).

2. Turn onto a floured surface; knead until smooth and elastic, about 6-8 minutes. Place in a greased bowl, turning once to grease top. Cover and let rise in a warm place until doubled, about 1 hour.

3. Punch dough down. Turn onto a lightly floured surface. Divide into 24 pieces; shape into balls. In a shallow bowl, combine sugar and orange peel; set aside 2 tablespoons. Dip balls in melted butter; roll in remaining sugar mixture. Arrange in a greased 10-in. fluted tube pan. Sprinkle with 1/4 cup almonds. Cover and let rise until doubled, about 30 minutes.

mixture into egg. Return all to the pan, whisking constantly; cook and stir over low heat until mixture reaches at least 160° and is slightly thickened. Keep warm.

2. In a large bowl, whisk the biscuit mix, egg, milk, molasses and spices just until smooth. Pour batter by 1/4 cupfuls onto a greased hot griddle. Turn when bubbles form on top of pancake; cook until second side is set. Serve with cream cheese and lemon sauce. **Yield:** 12 pancakes (about 1-1/2 cups sauce).

★ *Frothy Orange-Pineapple Cooler*

(Pictured on page 26)

My kids think they've gone to heaven when I say "yes" to seconds of this smoothie. I never hesitate because it's a wholesome and nutritious recipe. ~Deidre Fallavollita, Vienna, Virginia

> 2 cups unsweetened pineapple juice
> 1 cup (8 ounces) vanilla yogurt
> 1 can (6 ounces) frozen orange juice concentrate, thawed
> 2 small ripe bananas, cut into chunks
> 1/2 cup frozen unsweetened strawberries
> 1 drop coconut extract, optional

In a blender, combine all ingredients; cover and process on high until smooth. Pour into chilled glasses; serve immediately. **Yield:** 6 servings.

Pumpkin Spice Granola

Although you can certainly enjoy this granola as a snack, it also makes a wonderful topping for a fruit salad—and a great addition to a brunch buffet. Or, pour portions into colorful plastic bags, tie them with ribbons and give them to your coworkers for Christmas. ~Lynn Arrington, Grissom AFB, Indiana

> 7 cups old-fashioned oats
> 2 cups flaked coconut
> 1 cup coarsely chopped pecans
> 1 cup sliced almonds
> 1 cup unsalted sunflower kernels
> 3/4 cup vegetable oil
> 3/4 cup honey
> 1/2 cup water
> 2-1/2 teaspoons pumpkin pie spice
> 1 teaspoon salt
> 1 teaspoon almond extract

1. In a large bowl, combine the oats, coconut, pecans, almonds and sunflower kernels; set aside. In a small saucepan, combine the oil, honey, water, pumpkin pie spice and salt. Cook and stir over medium heat for 2-3 minutes or until heated through. Remove from the heat; stir in extract. Pour over oat mixture and toss to coat.

2. Transfer to two greased 15-in. x 10-in. x 1-in. baking pans. Bake at 300° for 45-50 minutes or until golden brown, stirring every 15 minutes. Cool on wire racks. Store in an airtight container. **Yield:** 13 cups.

★ *Apple Raisin Crepes*

I've been eating—and making—these delectable breakfast treats for as long as I can remember. They look impressive but are quick and easy to prepare. Heating the filled crepes a second time turns them golden brown and adds a wonderful crispness. ~Darlene Brenden, Salem, Oregon

> 1-1/2 cups all-purpose flour
> 1/4 cup sugar
> 1 cup milk
> 6 tablespoons water
> 1/4 cup vegetable oil
> 1 egg
> FILLING:
> 5 cups thinly sliced peeled tart apples
> 1 cup sugar
> 1/2 cup raisins
> 2 teaspoons ground cinnamon
> 1 tablespoon confectioners' sugar

1. For batter, in a small mixing bowl, combine flour and sugar. Add the milk, water, oil and egg; mix well. Cover and refrigerate for 1 hour.

2. In a large saucepan, combine the apples, sugar, raisins and cinnamon. Cook and stir over medium heat for 8-10 minutes or until apples are tender; set aside.

3. Heat a lightly greased 8-in. nonstick skillet; pour 3 tablespoons of batter into the center of skillet. Lift and tilt pan to evenly coat bottom. Cook until top appears dry; turn and cook 15-20 seconds longer. Remove to a wire rack. Repeat with remaining batter, greasing skillet as needed. When cool, stack crepes with waxed paper or paper towels in between.

4. With a slotted spoon, fill each crepe with 1/4 cup of apples; roll up. On a lightly greased griddle or in a large skillet, cook crepes over medium heat for 3-4 minutes on each side or until golden brown. Sprinkle with confectioners' sugar. Serve immediately with remaining sauce from apples. **Yield:** 1 dozen.

Apple Raisin Crepes

Strawberry-Pecan Yeast Rolls

These treats are so good! The strawberry filling, creamy glaze and crunchy nuts balance the sweet yeast rolls so perfectly. My family loves to eat them as much as I enjoy making them.
~Annie Thomas, Michigan, Mississippi

4 to 4-1/2 cups all-purpose flour
1 package (1/4 ounce) active dry yeast
1 teaspoon salt
1-1/2 cups milk
1 tablespoon vegetable oil
1 tablespoon honey
1 egg
FILLING:
1/4 cup butter, softened
2/3 cup strawberry preserves
1 tablespoon sugar
1/2 teaspoon ground cinnamon
GLAZE:
1 package (3 ounces) cream cheese, softened
1-3/4 cups confectioners' sugar
1/4 teaspoon almond extract
1 to 2 tablespoons milk
1/2 cup chopped pecans

1. In a large mixing bowl, combine 2 cups flour, yeast and salt. In a small saucepan, heat milk, oil and honey to 120°-130°. Add to dry ingredients; beat just until moistened. Add egg; beat until smooth. Stir in enough remaining flour to form a soft dough.

2. Turn onto a floured surface; knead until smooth and elastic, about 6-8 minutes. Place in a greased bowl, turning once to grease top. Cover and let rise in a warm place until doubled, about 1 hour.

3. Punch dough down; turn onto a lightly floured surface. Divide in half; roll each portion into a 15-in. x 10-in. rectangle. Spread butter to within 1/2 in. of edges; spread with strawberry preserves. Combine sugar and cinnamon; sprinkle over preserves.

4. Roll up jelly-roll style, starting with a long side; pinch seams to seal. Cut each roll into 12 slices. Place cut side down in two greased 15-in. x 10-in. x 1-in. baking pans. Cover and let rise until almost doubled, about 30 minutes.

5. Bake at 350° for 25-30 minutes or until golden brown. Cool for 20 minutes. For glaze, in a small mixing bowl, beat the cream cheese, confectioners' sugar and extract until smooth. Add enough milk to achieve desired consistency; drizzle over rolls. Sprinkle with pecans. **Yield:** 2 dozen.

★ Chicken 'n' Ham Frittata

Because my family is busy, we often gather for Sunday brunch to discuss plans for the upcoming week over servings of this hearty egg dish. It's colorful and special enough to prepare for holiday get-togethers, too.
~Ruth Allen, Hebron, Kentucky

1/2 cup chopped green onions
2 garlic cloves, minced
2 tablespoons vegetable oil
1-1/4 cups chopped yellow summer squash
1 cup chopped zucchini
1/2 cup chopped sweet yellow pepper
1/2 cup chopped sweet red pepper
1 teaspoon minced fresh gingerroot
2 cups cubed cooked chicken breast
1 cup chopped deli ham
6 eggs
3/4 cup mayonnaise
1/4 teaspoon prepared horseradish
1/4 teaspoon pepper
1 cup (4 ounces) shredded Monterey Jack cheese

1. In a large ovenproof skillet, saute the onions and garlic in oil for 1 minute. Add the yellow squash, zucchini, peppers and ginger; cook and stir for 8 minutes or until vegetables are crisp-tender. Add the chicken and ham; cook 1 minute longer or until heated through. Remove from the heat.

2. In a large bowl, whisk the eggs, mayonnaise, horseradish and pepper until blended. Pour into skillet. Bake, uncovered, at 350° for 25-30 minutes or until eggs are completely set. Sprinkle with cheese; cover and let stand for 5 minutes or until cheese is melted. **Yield:** 6 servings.

★ Spanish Fritters

These fried cinnamon-sugar goodies from the Country Woman Test Kitchen staff are best when fresh and hot. Try them with cups of coffee or hot chocolate. Don't be surprised if people start dunking...and then go back for more fritters.

1/2 cup water
1/2 cup milk
1 tablespoon vegetable oil
1/4 teaspoon salt
1 cup all-purpose flour
1 egg
1/4 teaspoon grated lemon peel
Additional oil for frying
1/2 cup sugar
1/4 teaspoon ground cinnamon

1. In a large saucepan, combine the water, milk, oil and salt. Bring to a boil over medium-high heat. Add flour all at once. Reduce heat to low; beat vigorously with a wooden spoon until mixture forms a stiff ball. Transfer to a large mixing bowl; let stand for 5 minutes.

2. Beat on medium-high speed for 1 minute or until the dough softens. Add egg and lemon peel; beat for 1-2 minutes. Set aside to cool.

3. In a deep skillet, heat 1 in. of oil to 375°. Insert a large star tip in a pastry bag; fill with dough. Holding the bag perpendicular to a baking sheet, pipe dough into 4-in. strips. Transfer strips to skillet and fry until golden brown on both sides. Drain on paper towels. Combine the sugar and cinnamon; sprinkle over fritters. Serve warm. **Yield:** about 1 dozen.

Spanish Fritters
Chicken 'n' Ham Frittata

Braided Wreath Bread
Apple Cinnamon Rolls (p. 35)

Festive Breads

★ Braided Wreath Bread

I make this attractive bread to celebrate Santa Lucia Day on December 13. This Swedish custom is the symbolic start of Christmas in Scandinavia, a festival of lights that brightens the short, dark days of winter. I position seven birthday candle holders in my braided loaf before adding candles to prevent wax from melting on top of the bread. ~Janet Uram, Willowick, Ohio

    1 package (1/4 ounce) active dry yeast
    1/4 cup warm water (110° to 115°)
    1/3 cup warm milk (110° to 115°)
    1/4 cup sugar
    1/4 cup butter, cubed
      2 eggs
      1 teaspoon grated orange peel
    1/2 teaspoon salt
    1/2 teaspoon orange extract
  2-1/2 to 3 cups all-purpose flour

1. In a large mixing bowl, dissolve yeast in warm water. Add the milk, sugar, butter, 1 egg, orange peel, salt, extract and 1 cup flour; beat until smooth. Stir in enough remaining flour to form a soft dough.

2. Turn onto a floured surface; knead until smooth and elastic, about 6-8 minutes. Place in a greased bowl, turning once to grease top. Cover and let rise in a warm place until doubled, about 1 hour.

3. Punch dough down; divide into thirds. Roll each portion into a 20-in. rope. Braid the ropes; shape into a wreath and pinch ends to seal. Place on a greased baking sheet. Cover and let rise in a warm place until doubled, about 45 minutes.

4. Beat the remaining egg; lightly brush over dough. Bake at 350° for 30-35 minutes or until golden brown. Cool for 10 minutes before removing from pan to a wire rack. **Yield:** 12 servings.

★ Frosted Carrot Mini Muffins

These delicate muffins, developed by the Country Woman home economists, feature the sweet goodness of carrots and coconut topped with rich, citrusy frosting. Young and old alike will love them and definitely ask for seconds...and thirds.

    1/4 cup butter, softened
    1/4 cup shortening
      6 tablespoons sugar
      1 egg
    1/2 cup mashed cooked carrots
    1/2 teaspoon vanilla extract
      1 cup all-purpose flour
      1 teaspoon baking powder
    1/4 teaspoon salt
      6 tablespoons flaked coconut, chopped
  FROSTING:
      2 tablespoons butter, softened
      1 cup confectioners' sugar
      1 teaspoon grated orange peel
    1/2 teaspoon orange juice
      1 to 2 teaspoons milk

1. In a large mixing bowl, cream the butter, shortening and sugar. Beat in the egg, carrots and vanilla. Combine the flour, baking powder and salt; gradually add to creamed mixture. Stir in coconut.

2. Fill greased or paper-lined miniature muffin cups three-fourths full. Bake at 400° for 12-14 minutes or until a toothpick comes out clean. Cool for 5 minutes before removing from pans to wire racks to cool completely.

3. For frosting, in a small mixing bowl, cream the butter, confectioners' sugar, orange peel and juice; add enough milk to achieve desired consistency. Spread over muffins. **Yield:** 2-1/2 dozen.

Frosted Carrot Mini Muffins

Banana Nut Fruitcake

⭐ Banana Nut Fruitcake

Combining two popular baked goods—banana bread and fruit-cake—yielded this treat. Even people who don't care for fruitcake will like this version! ~Brenda Williams, Silsbee, Texas

1-1/2 cups sugar
  3/4 cup vegetable oil
   2 eggs, lightly beaten
   1 teaspoon vanilla extract
1-1/2 cups mashed ripe bananas (about 3 medium)
   3 cups all-purpose flour
   1 teaspoon salt
   1 teaspoon baking soda
1-1/2 cups chopped pecans
   1 cup chopped candied cherries
  1/2 cup chopped candied pineapple

1. In a large mixing bowl, beat the sugar and oil. Beat in eggs and vanilla. Add bananas; mix well. Combine the flour, salt and baking soda; add to banana mixture just until blended. Fold in the pecans, cherries and pineapple.

2. Pour into two greased 8-in. x 4-in. x 2-in. loaf pans. Bake at 350° for 50-60 minutes or until golden brown and a toothpick inserted near the center comes out clean. Cool for 10 minutes before removing from pans to wire racks. **Yield:** 2 loaves.

Cranberry Pumpkin Bread

This is a fun way to use pumpkin and cranberries, two ingredients that pop up regularly on holiday menus. The bread has a fine texture and pretty color. ~Flo Burtnett, Gage, Oklahoma

4-1/2 cups all-purpose flour
4-1/2 cups sugar
   2 tablespoons plus 1-1/2 teaspoons pumpkin
    pie spice
   3 teaspoons baking soda
2-1/4 teaspoons salt
1-1/2 cups dried cranberries

ADDITIONAL INGREDIENTS (for *each* loaf):
   2 eggs
  3/4 cup canned pumpkin
  1/2 cup vegetable oil
  1/4 cup orange juice
GLAZE (optional):
   1 cup confectioners' sugar
   4 teaspoons milk

1. In a large bowl, combine the first six ingredients. Store in an airtight container in a cool dry place for up to 6 months. **Yield:** 3 batches (about 10-1/2 cups total).

2. To prepare bread: Place 3-1/2 cups mix in a large bowl. In another bowl, combine the eggs, pumpkin, oil and orange juice; stir into dry ingredients just until moistened.

3. Pour into a greased and floured 9-in. x 5-in. x 3-in. loaf pan. Bake at 350° for 60-65 minutes or until a toothpick inserted near the center comes out clean. Cool for 10 minutes before removing from pan to a wire rack to cool completely. If desired, combine glaze ingredients; drizzle over bread. **Yield:** 1 loaf.

   Editor's Note: Contents of mix may settle during storage. When preparing recipe, spoon mix into measuring cup.

Pecan Apple Kringle

My mother-in-law shared this pastry recipe with me a while back. Fresh from the oven, it makes a tasty Sunday breakfast when served with fresh fruit. ~Tammy Rowland, Unalaska, Alaska

   1 package (1/4 ounce) active dry yeast
  1/4 cup warm water (110° to 115°)
   2 cups all-purpose flour
4-1/2 teaspoons sugar
  1/2 teaspoon salt
  1/2 cup cold butter
  1/2 cup warm milk (110° to 115°)
   1 egg, *separated*
FILLING:
  3/4 cup finely chopped peeled apple
  1/2 cup packed brown sugar
  1/3 cup finely chopped pecans
GLAZE:
   1 cup confectioners' sugar
   4 teaspoons water
  1/2 teaspoon vanilla extract
   2 tablespoons chopped pecans

1. In a small bowl, dissolve yeast in warm water. In a large mixing bowl, combine the flour, sugar and salt; cut in butter until crumbly. Stir in the yeast mixture, milk and egg yolk; beat until smooth (dough will be very soft). Do not knead. Cover and refrigerate for 2 hours or overnight.

2. Punch dough down. Turn onto a well-floured surface; divide in half. Refrigerate one portion. Roll remaining portion into an 18-in. x 6-in. rectangle. In a small mixing bowl, beat egg white until stiff peaks form; brush half down the center of rectangle. Combine filling ingredients; sprinkle half over egg white.

3. Fold sides of dough over filling, overlapping by 1-1/2 in.; pinch seam to seal. Carefully place seam side down on an ungreased baking sheet. Shape into a horseshoe; pinch ends to seal. Repeat with remaining dough, egg white and filling. Cover and let rise in a warm place until doubled, about 35 minutes.

4. Bake at 400° for 18-22 minutes or until golden brown. Cool for 15 minutes before removing from pans to wire racks. For glaze, combine the confectioners' sugar, water and vanilla; spread over kringles. Sprinkle with pecans. **Yield:** 2 kringles.

★ Apple Cinnamon Rolls

(Pictured on page 32)

I like to serve these cinnamon rolls on Christmas morning. This recipe is great because it can be prepared a day early and makes big portions. ~Lynn Thomas, Lakewood, New York

    4-1/2 to 5 cups all-purpose flour
      1/3 cup sugar
        1 package (1/4 ounce) active dry yeast
      1/2 teaspoon salt
        1 cup milk
      1/3 cup butter, cubed
        3 eggs
FILLING:
      3/4 cup packed brown sugar
      1/4 cup all-purpose flour
        1 tablespoon ground cinnamon
      1/2 cup cold butter
        1 cup grated peeled apple
      1/2 cup chopped pecans
GLAZE:
        1 cup confectioners' sugar
        2 tablespoons milk

1. In a large mixing bowl, combine 2-1/4 cups flour, sugar, yeast and salt. In a saucepan, heat milk and butter to 120°-130°. Add to dry ingredients; beat just until moistened. Add eggs; beat until smooth. Stir in enough remaining flour to form a soft dough.

2. Turn onto a floured surface; knead until smooth and elastic, about 6-8 minutes. Place in a greased bowl, turning once to grease top. Cover and let rise in a warm place until doubled, about 1 hour.

3. In a bowl, combine the brown sugar, flour and cinnamon. Cut in butter until crumbly; set aside. Punch dough down. Turn onto a floured surface; let rest for 10 minutes. Roll into a 12-in. square. Sprinkle crumb mixture to within 1/2 in. of edges; top with apple and pecans.

4. Roll up jelly-roll style, starting with a long side; pinch seams to seal. Cut into 1-1/2-in. slices. Place cut side up in a greased 13-in. x 9-in. x 2-in. baking dish. Cover and refrigerate for 2 to 24 hours.

5. Uncover and let stand at room temperature for 30 minutes before baking. Bake at 350° for 30-35 minutes or until golden brown. Combine the glaze ingredients; drizzle over rolls. Serve warm. **Yield:** 9 rolls.

★ Toasted Sunflower Bread

Although I found this recipe in an old cookbook, the hearty flavor appeals to all generations. It's a nice alternative to ordinary whole wheat bread. ~Caroline Kunkel, St. Joseph, Missouri

    1-1/4 cups sunflower kernels, *divided*
        1 tablespoon soy sauce
        1 tablespoon active dry yeast
        3 cups warm water (110° to 115°)
        4 cups whole wheat flour
        1 tablespoon brown sugar
        1 tablespoon vegetable oil
        2 teaspoons salt
    2 to 2-1/2 cups all-purpose flour
        1 egg
        1 tablespoon cold water

1. In a small skillet over medium heat, cook and stir 1 cup of sunflower kernels until lightly browned, about 6 minutes; remove from the heat. Stir in soy sauce until kernels are evenly coated. Cool, stirring several times. Transfer to a blender or food processor; cover and process until ground.

2. In a large mixing bowl, dissolve yeast in warm water. Add the wheat flour, brown sugar, oil, salt and ground sunflower kernels; beat until smooth. Stir in enough all-purpose flour to form a firm dough.

3. Turn onto a floured surface; knead until smooth and elastic, about 5-7 minutes. Place in a greased bowl, turning once to grease top. Cover and let rise in a warm place until doubled, about 1 hour.

4. Punch dough down. Turn onto a floured surface; knead 10 times. Divide in half; let rest for 5 minutes. Sprinkle 3 tablespoons of sunflower kernels over the bottom and sides of two greased 8-in. x 4-in. x 2-in. loaf pans. Shape dough into loaves; place in pans. Press remaining kernels into top of dough. Cover and let rise until doubled, about 45 minutes.

5. Beat egg and cold water; brush over dough. Bake at 375° for 40-45 minutes or until golden brown. Remove from pans to wire racks to cool. **Yield:** 2 loaves.

Toasted Sunflower Bread

Pumpkin Dinner Rolls

Cranberry-Nut Coffee Cake

If you need a quick treat that will make a lasting impression, give this a try!   ~Lorraine Darocha, Berkshire, Massachusetts

    2 cups biscuit/baking mix
    2 tablespoons sugar
    1 egg
  2/3 cup milk
  1/2 cup chopped pecans *or* walnuts
  1/4 cup packed brown sugar
  1/4 teaspoon ground cinnamon
  2/3 cup whole-berry cranberry sauce
GLAZE:
    1 cup confectioners' sugar
    1 tablespoon water
  1/2 teaspoon vanilla extract

1. In a large bowl, combine the biscuit mix and sugar. Whisk the egg and milk; add to dry ingredients and mix well. Pour into a greased 9-in. square baking pan.

2. Combine the nuts, brown sugar and cinnamon; sprinkle over batter. Spoon cranberry sauce over the top.

3. Bake at 400° for 20-25 minutes or until a toothpick inserted near the center comes out clean. Combine the glaze ingredients; drizzle over warm coffee cake. **Yield:** 9 servings.

★Mocha-Cinnamon Coffee Ring

This tender coffee cake is so sweet and delightful, it doesn't need frosting.   ~Bette Mintz, Glendale, California

  3/4 cup chopped walnuts
  1/3 cup sugar
    1 tablespoon baking cocoa
    1 teaspoon instant coffee granules
    1 teaspoon ground cinnamon
BATTER:
  3/4 cup butter, softened
1-1/2 cups sugar
    4 eggs
    1 teaspoon vanilla extract
2-1/4 cups all-purpose flour
    2 teaspoons baking powder
    1 teaspoon baking soda
1-1/2 cups (12 ounces) sour cream
  1/2 cup semisweet chocolate chips

1. In a small bowl, combine the first five ingredients; set aside. In a large mixing bowl, cream butter and sugar. Add eggs, one at a time, beating well after each addition. Beat in vanilla. Combine the flour, baking powder and baking soda; add to creamed mixture alternately with sour cream. Stir in chocolate chips.

2. Pour a third of the batter into a greased 10-in. fluted tube pan. Sprinkle with half of the walnut mixture; repeat layers. Top with remaining batter. Bake at 350° for 40-45 minutes or until a toothpick comes out clean. Cool for 10 minutes before removing to a wire rack. **Yield:** 12-16 servings.

★Pumpkin Dinner Rolls

Serve these spicy-sweet pumpkin rolls for dinner—or any time of day—and get ready to hear a chorus of "yums" in your kitchen!
~Linnea Rein, Topeka, Kansas

  3/4 cup milk
  1/3 cup packed brown sugar
    5 tablespoons butter, *divided*
    1 teaspoon salt
    2 packages (1/4 ounce *each*) active dry yeast
  1/2 cup warm water (110° to 115°)
    2 to 2-1/2 cups all-purpose flour
1-1/2 cups whole wheat flour
  1/2 cup canned pumpkin
  1/2 teaspoon ground cinnamon
  1/4 teaspoon ground ginger
  1/4 teaspoon ground nutmeg

1. In a small saucepan, heat the milk, brown sugar, 4 tablespoons butter and salt to 110°-115°; set aside. In a large mixing bowl, dissolve yeast in warm water. Stir in the milk mixture. Add 1-1/2 cups all-purpose flour, wheat flour, pumpkin, cinnamon, ginger and nutmeg; beat until smooth. Add enough remaining all-purpose flour to form a soft dough.

2. Turn onto a floured surface; knead until smooth and elastic, about 6-8 minutes. Place in a greased bowl, turning once to grease top. Cover and let rise in a warm place until doubled, about 1 hour.

3. Punch dough down. Divide into 20 pieces; shape into balls. Place in a greased 13-in. x 9-in. x 2-in. baking pan. Cover and let rise for 30 minutes or until doubled.

4. Melt remaining butter; brush over dough. Bake at 375° for 20-25 minutes or until golden brown. Remove from pan to a wire rack. Serve warm. **Yield:** 20 rolls.

Mocha-Cinnamon Coffee Ring

Baked Onion Brie Spread (p. 40)
Sweet-and-Sour Sausages
Potato Salad Bites

Amazing Appetizers

★ Potato Salad Bites

These salad-filled potato skins are packed with the kind of down-home goodness everyone loves. Let them chill for a few hours to enhance the flavor. ~Stephanie Sheridan, Plainfield, Vermont

    10 small red potatoes
    1/4 cup chopped pimiento-stuffed olives
    2 teaspoons minced fresh parsley
    1 teaspoon finely chopped onion
    1/2 cup mayonnaise
    1-3/4 teaspoons Dijon mustard
    1/8 teaspoon pepper
    1/4 teaspoon salt
Paprika
Parsley sprigs, optional

1. Place the potatoes in a saucepan and cover with water. Bring to a boil. Reduce heat; cover and cook for 12-15 minutes or until tender. Drain and immediately place potatoes in ice water; drain and pat dry.

2. Peel two potatoes; finely dice and place in a small bowl. Cut the remaining potatoes in half. With a melon baller, scoop out pulp, leaving a 3/8-in. shell; set shells aside. Dice pulp and add to bowl. Stir in olives, parsley and onion. Combine mayonnaise, mustard and pepper; gently stir into potato mixture.

3. Sprinkle potato shells with salt; stuff with potato salad. Sprinkle with paprika. Chill for at least 1 hour before serving. Garnish with parsley if desired. **Yield:** 16 appetizers.

★ Sweet-and-Sour Sausages

A perfect buffet appetizer, these zesty links also make a great main course. I've prepared them so often that I can recite the recipe from memory. ~Dorothy Anderson, Langley, British Columbia

    2 packages (16 ounces each) miniature smoked
      sausages
    2 tablespoons butter
    1 can (15 ounces) sliced peaches, drained and halved
    1 cup chili sauce
    3/4 cup sugar
    1/2 cup ketchup
    1 teaspoon dried minced onion
    1 teaspoon curry powder

1. In a large skillet, brown sausages in butter. In a large bowl, combine the remaining ingredients; stir in the sausages. Transfer to a greased 2-qt. baking dish.

2. Bake, uncovered, at 350° for 30 minutes. Stir; bake 15 minutes longer or until bubbly. **Yield:** 18 servings.

★ Creamy Crab with Artichoke Dippers

The Northwest is famous for crab, and this appetizer recipe is easy yet elegant. ~Shirley Hewitt, Milwaukie, Oregon

    2 large artichokes
    2/3 cup mayonnaise
    2 tablespoons prepared mustard
    2 tablespoons chopped green onion
    2 teaspoons Worcestershire sauce
Dash hot pepper sauce
    3 cans (6 ounces each) crabmeat, drained, flaked and
      cartilage removed

1. Place artichokes upside down in a steamer basket; place the basket in a saucepan over 1 in. of water. Bring to a boil; cover and steam for 25-35 minutes or until tender. Remove artichokes from the basket; refrigerate until chilled.

2. Meanwhile, in a bowl, combine the mayonnaise, mustard, onion, Worcestershire sauce and hot pepper sauce; stir in crab. Cover and chill for several hours.

3. Just before serving, transfer crab dip to a serving bowl. Remove leaves from artichokes to use as dippers. **Yield:** 2 cups.

Creamy Crab with Artichoke Dippers

Special Cheese Balls

★ Special Cheese Balls

Coated with nuts, these cheese balls are impossible to pass up on a buffet table. I've even served them with crackers and fruit at morning meetings. ~Margaret Nichols, White Hall, Illinois

    2 packages (8 ounces *each*) cream cheese, softened
    2 cups (8 ounces) shredded sharp cheddar cheese
    2 cups (8 ounces) shredded mild cheddar cheese
    4 ounces crumbled blue cheese
4-1/2 teaspoons prepared horseradish
    1 teaspoon Worcestershire sauce
1/8 to 1/4 teaspoon onion powder
1/8 teaspoon garlic powder
1/3 cup finely chopped pecans, toasted
1/3 cup finely chopped salted peanuts
Assorted crackers, grapes *and/or* apple slices

1. In a large mixing bowl, combine the cheeses, horseradish, Worcestershire sauce, onion powder and garlic powder; beat until blended. Shape into two balls. Cover and refrigerate for 15 minutes.

2. Combine pecans and peanuts; press onto cheese balls. Cover and refrigerate for at least 2 hours. Serve with crackers, grapes and/or apple slices. **Yield:** 2 cheese balls (2 cups each).

Shrimp 'n' Snow Pea Wrap-Ups

This combination of zesty shrimp and crunchy peapods tastes as festive as it looks. I've served these wrap-ups at get-togethers many times. ~Earnestine Jackson, Beaumont, Texas

    1 cup oil and vinegar salad dressing
    1 garlic clove, minced
    1 teaspoon minced fresh gingerroot
    1 pound cooked medium shrimp, peeled and
        deveined (about 36)
    2 cups water
    4 ounces fresh snow peas (about 36)

1. In a large bowl, combine the salad dressing, ginger and garlic. Stir in shrimp; cover and refrigerate for 2 hours.

2. Meanwhile, in a small saucepan, bring water to a boil. Add snow peas; cover and boil for 1 minute. Drain and imme-

diately place peas in ice water; drain and pat dry.

3. Drain and discard marinade. Wrap a snow pea around each shrimp; secure with a toothpick. Chill until serving. **Yield:** about 3 dozen.

★ Baked Onion Brie Spread

(Pictured on page 38)

The buttery brie-and-onion flavor of this spread just melts in your mouth. Plus, you can even eat the bread bowl, which my husband says is the best part! ~Lori Adams, Mooresville, Indiana

    1 large onion, chopped
    2 tablespoons minced garlic
    2 tablespoons butter
    1 round (8 ounces) Brie *or* Camembert cheese, rind
        removed and cubed
    1 package (8 ounces) cream cheese, cubed
3/4 cup sour cream
    2 teaspoons brown sugar
    2 teaspoons lemon juice
    1 teaspoon Worcestershire sauce
1/8 teaspoon salt
1/8 teaspoon pepper
    1 round loaf (18 ounces) sourdough bread
Paprika
Fresh vegetables

1. In a large skillet, cook onion and garlic in butter over medium heat for 8-10 minutes or until onion is golden brown, stirring frequently. Remove from the heat; set aside.

2. Place Brie and cream cheese in a microwave-safe dish. Microwave, uncovered, on high for 2 minutes or until softened. Whisk in the sour cream, brown sugar, lemon juice, Worcestershire sauce, salt, pepper and onion mixture.

3. Cut top off loaf of bread; set aside. Hollow out loaf, leaving a 3/4-in. shell. Cut removed bread into cubes. Fill shell with cheese mixture; replace top. Wrap in a large piece of heavy-duty foil (about 18 in. square).

4. Bake at 400° for 1 hour or until spread is bubbly. Discard top of bread. Sprinkle paprika over spread. Serve with bread cubes and vegetables. **Yield:** 2-3/4 cups.

Reuben Appetizers

Each year, I collect appetizer recipes to make for the annual Christmas party we throw for friends and family. These tidbits are always a big hit. ~Pat Bohn, Oregon City, Oregon

1/2 cup Thousand Island salad dressing
    4 plain bagels, split
    2 to 3 large dill pickles, sliced lengthwise
    1 pound thinly sliced corned beef
    8 slices Swiss cheese

Spread salad dressing on each bagel half. Top with pickle slices, corned beef and cheese. Place on an ungreased baking sheet. Broil 6 in. from the heat for 4-6 minutes or until cheese is melted. Cut each into six wedges; serve immediately. **Yield:** 4 dozen.

Hot Spiced Cranberry Punch

You'll love having this punch at your next get-together. Its sweet-tart flavor, spices and dash of citrus can't be beat.
~Geraldine Evans, Hermosa, South Dakota

    8 cups cranberry juice
2-2/3 cups water
1-1/3 cups sugar
  16 whole cloves
   1 teaspoon ground cinnamon
1/2 to 1 teaspoon ground nutmeg
2/3 cup orange juice
1/2 cup lemon juice

1. In a Dutch oven or large saucepan, combine the cranberry juice, water and sugar; bring to a boil over medium heat. Place cloves on a double thickness of cheesecloth; bring up corners of cloth and tie with string to form a bag. Add the cinnamon, nutmeg and spice bag to the pan. Reduce heat; simmer, uncovered, for 20 minutes.

2. Discard spice bag. Stir in the orange and lemon juices. Transfer to a slow cooker; keep warm. **Yield:** 12 servings (3 quarts).

Tropical Dip

This yummy, island-inspired dip from the Country Woman Test Kitchen staff bursts with pineapple and coconut.

    1 can (8 ounces) crushed pineapple, undrained
    1 package (3.4 ounces) instant coconut cream pudding mix
3/4 cup cold milk
1/2 cup sour cream
Flaked coconut, toasted
Assorted fresh fruit

In a blender or food processor, combine the pineapple, pudding mix, milk and sour cream; cover and process for 30 seconds. Transfer to a serving bowl; cover and refrigerate for 30 minutes. Garnish with toasted coconut. Serve with fruit. **Yield:** 2 cups.

★ Cajun Canapes

I came across these filled biscuits at a party—and now they're a family-favorite snack. ~Jerri Peachee, Gentry, Arkansas

    2 cans (12 ounces *each*) refrigerated buttermilk biscuits
1/2 pound bulk pork sausage, cooked and drained
1-1/2 cups (6 ounces) shredded cheddar cheese
1/4 cup chopped green pepper
1/4 cup mayonnaise
    2 green onions, chopped
    2 teaspoons lemon juice
1/2 teaspoon salt
1/2 teaspoon paprika
1/4 teaspoon garlic powder
1/4 teaspoon dried thyme
1/8 to 1/4 teaspoon cayenne pepper

1. Bake biscuits according to package directions, except turn biscuits over halfway through baking. Remove from pans to wire racks to cool completely.

2. Using a melon baller, scoop out center of each biscuit, leaving a 3/8-in. shell (discard biscuit center or save for another use).

3. In a bowl, combine the remaining ingredients. Spoon about 1 tablespoonful into the center of each biscuit. Place on an ungreased baking sheet. Bake at 400° for 8-10 minutes or until heated through. Serve warm. **Yield:** 20 appetizers.

Bacon-Pecan Stuffed Mushrooms

When I had some kitchen remodeling done a few years ago, this recipe disappeared. But I'd shared it so often that I had no trouble getting a copy. ~Beverly Pierce, Indianola, Mississippi

    1 pound large fresh mushrooms
    4 tablespoons butter, *divided*
    2 tablespoons vegetable oil
1/4 teaspoon salt
    2 tablespoons finely chopped onion
    1 cup soft bread crumbs
    6 bacon strips, cooked and crumbled
    2 tablespoons chopped pecans
    2 tablespoons sherry *or* beef broth
    2 tablespoons sour cream
    2 tablespoons minced chives

1. Remove mushroom stems (discard or save for another use). In a large skillet, heat 2 tablespoons butter and oil over medium-high heat. Saute mushroom caps for 2 minutes on each side; sprinkle with salt. Remove with a slotted spoon to paper towels.

2. In the same skillet, saute the onion in remaining butter until tender. Remove from the heat; stir in the remaining ingredients.

3. Spoon into mushroom caps. Place on a broiler pan; broil 5 in. from the heat for 2-3 minutes or until filling is browned. Serve warm. **Yield:** 12-14 appetizers.

Cajun Canapes

Make-Ahead Mashed Potatoes (p. 44)
Rib Roast with Madeira Gravy

Merry Dinner Delights

⭐ Rib Roast with Madeira Gravy

I discovered this recipe years ago, and it proved to be such a winner that I still enjoy serving it to family and friends during the holidays. ~Isabell Cooper, Cambridge, Nova Scotia

      2 teaspoons salt
1-1/4 teaspoons ground thyme
      1 teaspoon pepper
      1 boneless beef rib roast (7 to 8 pounds)
GRAVY:
   1/2 pound sliced fresh mushrooms
   1/2 cup finely chopped onion
      2 tablespoons tomato paste
      3 to 3-1/2 cups beef broth
   1/4 cup all-purpose flour
   1/2 cup Madeira wine *or* additional beef broth
      2 tablespoons lemon juice
Salt and pepper to taste

1. Combine the salt, thyme and pepper; rub over roast. Place fat side up on a rack in a shallow roasting pan. Bake, uncovered, at 350° for 3 hours or until meat reaches desired doneness (for medium-rare, a meat thermometer should read 145°; medium, 160°; well-done, 170°). Transfer to a warm serving platter. Let stand for 20 minutes.

2. Meanwhile, for gravy, pour pan drippings and loosened browned bits into a 4-cup measuring cup. Skim fat, reserving 1/4 cup; set drippings aside. In a skillet, saute the mushrooms and onion in reserved fat until tender. Add tomato paste; cook and stir until combined. Remove from the heat.

3. Add enough beef broth to reserved drippings to measure 3-1/2 cups. In a large saucepan, combine the flour, wine, lemon juice and broth mixture until smooth. Stir in mushroom mixture. Bring to a boil; cook and stir for 2 minutes or until thickened. Season with salt and pepper. Slice roast and serve with gravy. **Yield:** 14-16 servings.

⭐ Italian Cheese Sesame Rolls

These rolls are my family's favorite. Everyone from our children to our great-grandchildren dig right in when I put these goodies on the table. ~Jacki Lesandrini, Crystal Falls, Michigan

      1 package (1/4 ounce) active dry yeast
   3/4 cup warm water (110° to 115°)
      4 to 4-1/2 cups all-purpose flour
   1/4 cup sugar
      1 teaspoon salt
   1/4 cup cold butter, cubed
      1 egg, lightly beaten
   3/4 cup warm milk (110° to 115°)
FILLING:
      2 tablespoons butter, softened
      2 teaspoons garlic powder
   3/4 cup shredded mozzarella cheese
TOPPING:
      1 egg
      1 tablespoon water
      1 tablespoon sesame seeds

1. In a small bowl, dissolve yeast in warm water. In a large mixing bowl, combine 3-1/2 cups flour, sugar and salt. Cut in butter until crumbly. Combine egg and warm milk; add to the crumb mixture. Stir in yeast mixture; beat until smooth. Add enough remaining flour to form a firm dough.

2. Turn onto a lightly floured surface; knead until smooth and elastic, about 5-7 minutes. Place in a greased bowl, turning once to grease top. Cover and let rise in a warm place until doubled, about 1 hour.

3. Punch dough down. Turn onto a lightly floured surface; divide in half. Roll each portion into a 12-in. circle. Spread with butter; sprinkle with garlic powder and cheese. Cut each into 12 wedges. Roll up wedges from a wide end and place point side down on greased baking sheets.

4. In a small bowl, beat egg and water. Brush over dough. Sprinkle with sesame seeds. Cover and let rise in a warm place until doubled, about 40 minutes. Bake at 350° for 16-18 minutes or until golden brown. Remove to wire racks. **Yield:** 2 dozen.

Italian Cheese Sesame Rolls

Chocolate-Swirl Eggnog Pie

★ Chocolate-Swirl Eggnog Pie

My mom has been collecting recipes for 25 years, and her file is huge. Before I got married, I copied down all my favorites, including this creamy pie. ~Angela Goodman, Moscow, Idaho

    1 cup all-purpose flour
  3/4 cup finely chopped walnuts
  1/4 cup packed brown sugar
  1/3 cup butter, melted
    3 tablespoons semisweet chocolate chips, melted
FILLING:
  1/2 cup sugar
    2 tablespoons cornstarch
    2 cups eggnog
    1 envelope unflavored gelatin
  1/4 cup cold water
  3/4 teaspoon rum extract
  1/4 cup semisweet chocolate chips, melted
    1 cup heavy whipping cream, whipped

1. In a bowl, combine the flour, walnuts, brown sugar, butter and chocolate. Press into a 9-in. pie plate. Bake at 375° for 12-15 minutes or until set. Cool completely on a wire rack.

2. For filling, in a small saucepan, combine the sugar and cornstarch. Stir in eggnog until smooth. Cook and stir over medium-high heat until thickened and bubbly. Reduce heat; cook and stir 2 minutes longer. Remove from the heat.

3. In a small bowl, sprinkle gelatin over cold water; let stand for 1 minute. Stir into eggnog mixture until gelatin is dissolved. Divide mixture in half. Stir rum extract into one half; fold chocolate into the other half. Cover and refrigerate until partially set.

4. Fold cream into rum-flavored filling; spoon into crust. Spoon chocolate filling over the top; cut through with a knife to swirl the chocolate. Cover and refrigerate for at least 2 hours before serving. **Yield:** 8 servings.

    Editor's Note: This recipe was tested with commercially prepared eggnog.

★ Make-Ahead Mashed Potatoes

(Pictured on page 42)

Remember whipping up potatoes at the last minute before holiday meals? Never again! These are the most delicious mashed spuds we've ever tasted—but best of all, you make them the day before the feast. ~Marion Lowery, Medford, Oregon

  12 medium potatoes, peeled and quartered
    1 package (8 ounces) cream cheese, softened
  1/3 cup sour cream
    5 tablespoons butter, softened
1-1/4 teaspoons salt
    1 teaspoon paprika
  1/2 teaspoon pepper
  1/4 cup minced chives, optional
    2 tablespoons milk

1. Place the potatoes in a large saucepan and cover with water. Bring to a boil. Reduce heat; cover and cook for 15-20 minutes or until tender. Drain.

2. In a large mixing bowl, beat cream cheese and sour cream until smooth. Add potatoes; beat until light and fluffy. Beat in the butter, salt, paprika, pepper and chives if desired. Spoon into a greased 2-1/2-qt. microwave-safe dish. Cover and refrigerate overnight.

3. Remove from the refrigerator 30 minutes before baking. Microwave, uncovered, on high for 10 minutes, stirring once. Stir in milk. Microwave 5 minutes longer or until heated through. **Yield:** 12 servings.

    Editor's Note: This recipe was tested in a 1,100-watt microwave.

Chicken Veggie Strudel

I serve this hearty entree often at dinner parties and usually keep a few extra strudels in the freezer in case company unexpectedly shows up. ~Debra McKim, Hastings, Nebraska

    3 cups cubed cooked chicken
    3 cups broccoli florets
    3 cups cauliflowerets
    3 cups diced carrots
    2 cups (8 ounces) shredded cheddar cheese
    2 cups (8 ounces) shredded Swiss cheese
    1 cup chopped onion
    3 eggs
    2 garlic cloves, minced
    2 tablespoons minced fresh parsley
    2 teaspoons *each* dried basil, tarragon and thyme
    2 teaspoons pepper
    2 tablespoons plus 1-1/2 cups butter, *divided*
    2 tablespoons all-purpose flour
    1 cup milk
    1 package (16 ounces) frozen phyllo dough
      (18-inch x 14-inch sheets)
    1 package (15 ounces) seasoned bread crumbs

1. In a large bowl, combine the first seven ingredients. In a small bowl, beat the eggs. Stir in the garlic, parsley, basil, tarragon, thyme and pepper. Add to chicken mixture; toss to coat. In a small saucepan, melt 2 tablespoons butter. Stir in flour until smooth; gradually stir in milk. Bring to a boil; cook and stir for 2 minutes or until thickened. Pour over chicken mixture; toss to coat.

2. Melt remaining butter. Place one sheet of phyllo dough on a work surface (keep remaining dough covered with plastic wrap and a damp towel to avoid drying out). Brush with butter; sprinkle with bread crumbs. Repeat layers five times.

3. Spread 5 cups of filling down the center of dough to within 1 in. of edges. Fold short sides 1 in. over filling. Roll up jelly-roll style, starting with a long side. Brush with butter. Place seam side down in an ungreased 15-in. x 10-in. x 1-in. baking pan.

4. Make two more strudels with remaining phyllo, butter and filling. Bake at 375° for 35-40 minutes or until golden brown. **Yield:** 3 loaves (8 servings each).

★ Cranberry Sorbet

(Pictured on page 47)

This sorbet's sweet-tart taste is so refreshing after a hearty meal. My mother made a batch at least once a year, either for Thanksgiving or Christmas. ~Ellen Glover, Clarkston, Washington

1 envelope unflavored gelatin
2-1/4 cups water, *divided*
4 cups fresh *or* frozen cranberries
2 cups sugar
2 cups ginger ale, chilled

1. In a small bowl, sprinkle gelatin over 1/4 cup water; set aside. In a large saucepan, bring cranberries and remaining water to a boil. Reduce heat; cook until berries pop. Remove from the heat; press cranberries through a sieve or food mill, reserving juice. Discard pulp.

2. In a bowl, combine the warm juice, gelatin and sugar until dissolved. Cool to room temperature. Stir in ginger ale. Pour into a freezer-proof mixing bowl; cover and place in the freezer until mixture is partially frozen. Beat with an electric mixer until light in color. Cover and freeze overnight. **Yield:** 12 servings.

Apple Sweet Potato Bake

This side dish is a winner. Not only do I like the flavor, I love the fact that it's easy. ~Valerie Walker, Canton, Illinois

2-1/2 pounds sweet potatoes
1/2 cup packed brown sugar
1/3 cup chopped walnuts
1 teaspoon ground cinnamon
1/8 teaspoon salt
3 cups thinly sliced peeled tart apples
4 tablespoons butter, *divided*

1. Place the sweet potatoes in a large saucepan and cover with water. Bring to a boil. Reduce heat; cover and simmer for 30 minutes or until tender. Drain. When cool enough to handle, peel potatoes and cut into 1/2-in. slices.

2. In a small bowl, combine the brown sugar, walnuts, cinnamon and salt; set aside. In a large skillet, saute apples in 2 tablespoons butter for 3-4 minutes or until tender. In a greased 1-1/2-qt. baking dish, layer half of the sweet potatoes, apples and brown sugar mixture. Repeat layers.

3. Dot with remaining butter. Cover and bake at 375° for 30 minutes. Uncover; bake 15 minutes longer or until bubbly. **Yield:** 6-8 servings.

★ Cream of Asparagus Soup

Kids may not want to try a vegetable soup, but once they spoon up a mouthful of this cheesy variety, the flavor will keep them coming back for more. ~Muriel Lerdal, Humboldt, Iowa

2 packages (12 ounces *each*) frozen cut asparagus
1/4 cup butter
2 tablespoons all-purpose flour
4 cups milk
1 cup (4 ounces) shredded Monterey Jack cheese
4 to 5 drops hot pepper sauce
1-1/2 teaspoons salt
3/4 to 1 teaspoon pepper

1. Prepare asparagus according to package directions; drain and set aside. In a large saucepan, melt butter. Stir in flour until smooth; gradually add milk. Bring to a boil; cook and stir for 2 minutes or until thickened. Cool slightly.

2. Pour half of the milk mixture into a blender; add half of the asparagus. Cover and process until blended. Strain and discard pulp; return soup to the saucepan. Repeat with the remaining milk mixture and asparagus. Stir in the cheese, hot pepper sauce, salt and pepper; heat through (do not boil). **Yield:** 6 servings.

Cream of Asparagus Soup

Roasted Peppers 'n' Cauliflower

★ Roasted Peppers 'n' Cauliflower

Roasting really enhances the taste of this cauliflower-red pepper-onion dish. The nicely seasoned veggies are great with nearly any main course. ~Cheryl Maczko, Reedville, West Virginia

  1 medium head cauliflower, broken into florets
  2 medium sweet red peppers, cut into strips
  2 small onions, cut into wedges
  2 tablespoons olive oil
1/2 teaspoon salt
1/2 teaspoon pepper
  1 tablespoon grated Parmesan cheese
  1 tablespoon minced fresh parsley

1. Place the cauliflower, red peppers and onions in a shallow roasting pan. Add the oil, salt and pepper; toss to coat. Bake, uncovered, at 425° for 20 minutes.

2. Stir; bake 10 minutes longer or until vegetables are tender and lightly browned. Transfer to a serving bowl; sprinkle with Parmesan cheese and parsley. **Yield:** 6 servings.

★ Cranberry-Stuffed Crown Roast of Pork

This is my favorite party roast—everyone just loves it! It makes such a statement when you place it on the table, and the flavor is incredible. ~Gloria Warczak, Cedarburg, Wisconsin

  1 teaspoon sugar
1/2 teaspoon dried thyme
1/2 teaspoon pepper
  1 pork crown roast (12 ribs and 7 pounds)
STUFFING:
3/4 cup chopped celery
1/2 cup chopped onion
1/4 cup butter
  5 cups cubed day-old bread
  1 cup chicken broth
2/3 cup cooked long grain rice

1/2 cup cooked wild rice
1/3 cup chopped fresh cranberries
1/4 cup minced fresh parsley
  2 tablespoons brown sugar
  1 tablespoon Worcestershire sauce
  2 teaspoons poultry seasoning
1/2 teaspoon pepper
CRANBERRY GRAVY:
  1 cup hot water
  3 tablespoons all-purpose flour
  1 teaspoon brown sugar
1/8 teaspoon dried marjoram
1/8 teaspoon pepper
1/2 cup cranberry juice

1. Combine sugar, thyme and pepper; rub over roast. Place on a rack in a large shallow roasting pan. Cover ends with foil. Bake at 350° for 2 hours.

2. In a skillet, saute celery and onion in butter until tender. In a large bowl, combine bread cubes and broth. Stir in the long grain rice, wild rice, cranberries, parsley, brown sugar, Worcestershire sauce, poultry seasoning, pepper and celery mixture.

3. Carefully spoon stuffing into center of roast. Bake 1 hour longer or until a meat thermometer reads 160°. Remove foil from ends; cover and let stand for 10-15 minutes.

4. Pour pan drippings and loosened browned bits into a 2-cup measuring cup; skim fat. Add enough hot water to measure 1-1/4 cups. In a small saucepan, combine the flour, brown sugar, marjoram, pepper and cranberry juice until blended. Gradually stir in drippings. Bring to a boil; cook and stir for 2 minutes or until thickened.

5. Remove stuffing to a bowl and cut between ribs. Serve with gravy. **Yield:** 12 servings.

★ Greens and Mushrooms With Raspberry Dressing

With a glistening red dressing and light flavor, this crisp salad is perfect for the holidays. It's a must-have on our Christmastime menus. ~Margery Richmond, Fort Collins, Colorado

1/4 cup cranberry juice
1/4 cup seedless raspberry jam
1/4 cup vegetable oil
  3 tablespoons white vinegar
1/4 teaspoon pepper
1/4 teaspoon salt
  8 to 10 cups torn mixed salad greens
1-1/2 cups sliced fresh mushrooms

1. For dressing, in a jar with a tight-fitting lid, combine the first six ingredients; shake well. Cover and refrigerate for at least 1 hour.

2. Just before serving, combine the salad greens and mushrooms in a large bowl. Shake dressing and pour over salad; toss to coat. **Yield:** 6-8 servings.

Greens and Mushrooms with Raspberry Dressing
Cranberry-Stuffed Crown Roast of Pork
Cranberry Sorbet (p. 45)

Ricotta Cheesecake (p. 50)
Luscious Lemon Angel Roll

Desserts That Dazzle

★ Luscious Lemon Angel Roll

I came across this recipe while preparing for a party and was thrilled with how easy it was to make. My guests were impressed that I could use a few simple ingredients to create such a stylish dessert. ~Pamela Wright, St. Helens, Oregon

1 package (16 ounces) angel food cake mix
3/4 cup confectioners' sugar, *divided*
1 package (8 ounces) cream cheese, softened
1 tablespoon lemon juice
2 teaspoons grated lemon peel
6 to 8 drops yellow food coloring, optional
1 carton (8 ounces) frozen whipped topping, thawed, *divided*
1 jar (11-3/4 ounces) strawberry ice cream topping, *divided*
Additional confectioners' sugar
12 fresh strawberries

1. Line a greased 15-in. x 10-in. x 1-in. baking pan with parchment paper; set aside. Prepare cake batter according to package directions. Spread evenly in prepared pan. Bake at 350° for 30-35 minutes or until cake springs back when lightly touched (cake will rise above edges of pan). Cool for 5 minutes.

2. Sprinkle 2 tablespoons confectioners' sugar over a kitchen towel. Invert cake onto towel; gently peel off parchment paper. Sprinkle with 2 tablespoons confectioners' sugar. Roll up cake in the towel jelly-roll style, starting with a short side. Cool completely on a wire rack.

3. In a small mixing bowl, beat cream cheese, lemon juice and peel, food coloring if desired and remaining confectioners' sugar until smooth. Fold in 1 cup whipped topping. Unroll cake. Spread 1/3 cup strawberry topping to within 1 in. of edges. Spread cream cheese mixture over topping. Roll up again. Place seam side down on a serving platter. Cover and refrigerate for 1 hour.

4. Dust with additional confectioners' sugar. Cut into slices; garnish with berries and remaining strawberry topping and whipped topping. Refrigerate leftovers. **Yield:** 12 servings.

★ Cream Puff Dessert

Inspired by classic cream puffs, this recipe is a wonderful treat. I've served it at Cub Scout banquets, birthday parties and holidays. I'm a regular baker, and this dessert is one of my all-time favorites. ~Denise Wahl, Lockport, Illinois

1 cup water
1/2 cup butter
1/4 teaspoon salt
1 cup all-purpose flour
4 eggs
FILLING:
1 package (8 ounces) cream cheese, softened
2-1/2 cups cold milk
2 packages (3.4 ounces *each*) instant vanilla pudding mix
TOPPING:
1 carton (8 ounces) frozen whipped topping, thawed
Chocolate syrup

1. In a saucepan over medium heat, bring the water, butter and salt to a boil. Add flour all at once and stir until a smooth ball forms. Continue beating until smooth and shiny. Remove from the heat; let stand for 5 minutes. Add the eggs, one at a time, beating well after each addition.

2. Pour into a greased 15-in. x 10-in. x 1-in. baking pan. Bake at 400° for 28-30 minutes or until puffed and golden brown. Cool on a wire rack.

3. For filling, in a large mixing bowl, beat the cream cheese, milk and pudding mixes until smooth. Spread over the crust; refrigerate for 20 minutes. Spread with whipped topping. Store in the refrigerator. Just before serving, drizzle with chocolate syrup. **Yield:** 15 servings.

Cream Puff Dessert

White Chocolate Christmas Torte

4. For frosting, in a small saucepan, melt white chocolate over very low heat. Cool for 10 minutes, stirring occasionally. In a large mixing bowl, beat cream cheese and butter. Gradually beat in melted chocolate and extracts. Gradually beat in confectioners' sugar until smooth.

5. To assemble, spread 2 tablespoons of jam over one cake layer; spread with 1/2 cup frosting. Repeat layers twice. Spread remaining frosting over top and sides of torte. Warm remaining jam; drizzle over dessert plates. Top with a slice of torte. **Yield:** 12-15 servings.

★Ricotta Cheesecake

(Pictured on page 48)

When I was a nurse, my coworkers and I regularly swapped recipes during lunch breaks. This creamy cheesecake was one of the best I received. ~Georgiann Franklin, Canfield, Ohio

> 1-1/4 cups graham cracker crumbs
>   3 tablespoons sugar
>   1/3 cup butter, melted
> **FILLING:**
>   2 cartons (15 ounces *each*) ricotta cheese
>   1 cup sugar
>   3 eggs, lightly beaten
>   2 tablespoons all-purpose flour
>   1 teaspoon vanilla extract

1. In a bowl, combine the graham cracker crumbs and sugar; stir in butter. Press onto the bottom and 1 in. up the sides of a greased 9-in. springform pan. Place on a baking sheet. Bake at 400° for 6-8 minutes or until crust is lightly browned around the edges. Cool on a wire rack.

2. In a large mixing bowl, beat ricotta cheese on medium speed for 1 minute. Add sugar; beat for 1 minute. Add eggs; beat just until combined. Beat in flour and vanilla. Pour into crust.

3. Place pan on a baking sheet. Bake at 350° for 50-60 minutes or until center is almost set. Cool on a wire rack for 10 minutes. Carefully run a knife around edge of pan to loosen; cool 1 hour longer. Refrigerate overnight. Remove sides of pan. Refrigerate leftovers. **Yield:** 12 servings.

White Chocolate Christmas Torte

Talk about a scene-stealer! This raspberry-filled cake, an exceptional dessert for any meal, is an especially lovely ending for a holiday feast. ~Carol Gillespie, Chambersburg, Pennsylvania

> 1-1/2 cups butter, cubed
>   3/4 cup water
>   4 squares (1 ounce *each*) white baking chocolate, chopped
> 1-1/2 cups buttermilk
>   4 eggs, lightly beaten
>   1 teaspoon vanilla extract
>   1/4 teaspoon rum extract
> 3-1/2 cups all-purpose flour, *divided*
>   1 cup chopped pecans, toasted
> 2-1/4 cups sugar
> 1-1/2 teaspoons baking soda
> **WHITE CHOCOLATE CREAM FROSTING:**
>   4 squares (1 ounce *each*) white baking chocolate, chopped
>   2 packages (one 8 ounces, one 3 ounces) cream cheese, softened
>   1/2 cup butter, softened
>   1 teaspoon vanilla extract
>   1/4 teaspoon rum extract
>   6 cups confectioners' sugar
>   1 cup seedless raspberry jam, *divided*

1. In a large saucepan, combine butter, water and white chocolate; cook and stir over low heat until melted. Remove from the heat; stir in the buttermilk, eggs and extracts.

2. In a small bowl, combine 1/2 cup flour and pecans. In a large mixing bowl, combine the sugar, baking soda and remaining flour. Gradually beat in butter mixture. Stir in pecan mixture.

3. Pour into three greased and floured 9-in. round baking pans. Bake at 350° for 25-30 minutes or until a toothpick inserted near the center comes out clean. Cool for 10 minutes before removing from pans to wire racks to cool completely.

Cran-Raspberry Gelatin Dessert

My sister-in-law served this gelatin on Christmas. I don't usually like cranberry sauce, but the sweetness of the raspberries made this dessert delicious. ~Lisa Rasmussen, Petoskey, Michigan

> 2 packages (3 ounces *each*) raspberry gelatin
> 2 cups boiling water
> 1 can (16 ounces) jellied cranberry sauce
> 1 package (10 ounces) frozen sweetened raspberries
> 1 tablespoon lemon juice
> 1 cup (8 ounces) sour cream
> 1 carton (8 ounces) frozen whipped topping, thawed

1. In a large mixing bowl, dissolve gelatin in boiling water. Add cranberry sauce, raspberries and lemon juice; beat on low speed until combined. Pour into a 3-qt. serving dish. Refrigerate for 8 hours or until set.

2. Just before serving, place the sour cream in a large bowl; fold in whipped topping. Spread over gelatin. **Yield:** 12 servings.

Pumpkin Chiffon Dessert

A nice alternative to traditional pie, this layered pumpkin dessert is a big hit during the holidays. I get many requests to bring it to gatherings. ~Martha Stine, Johnstown, Pennsylvania

  1-3/4 cups graham cracker crumbs
    1/4 cup sugar
    1/2 cup butter, melted
FILLING:
    1 package (8 ounces) cream cheese, softened
    3/4 cup sugar
    2 eggs
TOPPING:
    2 cups cold milk
    2 packages (3.4 ounces *each*) instant vanilla pudding mix
    1 can (15 ounces) solid-pack pumpkin
    1/4 teaspoon ground cinnamon
    1 carton (8 ounces) frozen whipped topping, thawed, *divided*
    1/4 cup chopped pecans, optional

1. In a bowl, combine the graham cracker crumbs, sugar and butter. Press into an ungreased 13-in. x 9-in. x 2-in. baking dish. Refrigerate for 30 minutes.

2. In a small mixing bowl, beat cream cheese and sugar until smooth. Beat in eggs. Spoon over crust. Bake at 350° for 18-22 minutes or until edges are lightly browned and center is set. Cool completely on a wire rack.

3. In a large mixing bowl, beat milk and pudding mixes for 2 minutes. Beat in pumpkin and cinnamon. Fold in 1 cup whipped topping. Spread over filling. Carefully spread with remaining whipped topping. Sprinkle with pecans if desired. Cover and refrigerate for at least 1 hour before serving. **Yield:** 12-16 servings.

★ Mile-High Peppermint Pie

The blend of chocolate and peppermint in this pie is simply divine—and so is the frothy meringue topping and rich fudge sauce I drizzle over each slice! ~Nancy Larkin, Maitland, Florida

  1-1/2 cups crushed chocolate-covered mint cookies
    2 tablespoons butter, melted
    5 cups peppermint ice cream, softened
CHOCOLATE SAUCE:
    1 square (1 ounce) semisweet baking chocolate, chopped
    1 tablespoon butter
    1/2 cup sugar
    3 tablespoons water

    2 tablespoons light corn syrup
    1/8 teaspoon salt
    1/2 teaspoon vanilla extract
MERINGUE:
    5 egg whites
  10 tablespoons sugar

1. Combine cookie crumbs and butter; press onto the bottom and up the sides of a 9-in. pie plate. Cover and freeze for 1 hour or until firm. Spread ice cream into crust. Cover and freeze until firm.

2. Shortly before serving, combine chocolate and butter in a small saucepan. Cook and stir over medium-low heat until melted. Stir in the sugar, water, corn syrup and salt. Bring to a boil. Reduce heat; simmer for 5 minutes or until sugar is dissolved, stirring frequently. Remove from the heat; stir in vanilla. Keep warm.

3. In a heavy saucepan over low heat, beat the egg whites and sugar on low speed with a portable mixer until mixture reaches 160°. Remove from the heat; transfer to a mixing bowl. Beat on high speed until stiff peaks form. Spread over frozen pie. Bake at 450° for 3 minutes or until meringue is lightly browned. Serve immediately with warm chocolate sauce. **Yield:** 8 servings.

Hot Cherry Sauce

This sweet-tart cherry sauce with a hint of cloves is just delightful. I use it with ham, but it also works beautifully as a dessert sauce. ~Noreen Martinac, Stevensville, Montana

  2 cans (14-1/2 ounces *each*) pitted tart cherries
  1 cup sugar
  1/4 cup cornstarch
  1/4 to 1/2 teaspoon ground cloves
  1 to 2 drops red food coloring, optional

Drain cherries, reserving juice; set cherries aside. In a large saucepan, combine the sugar, cornstarch and cloves; whisk in reserved cherry juice. Bring to a boil; cook and stir for 2 minutes or until thickened. Remove from the heat; stir in cherries and food coloring if desired. **Yield:** about 3-1/2 cups.

Mile-High Peppermint Pie

French Cream with Sugared Grapes

ter; surround with sugared grapes. **Yield:** 6 servings.

Editor's Note: Reduced-fat or fat-free sour cream and cream cheese are not recommended for this recipe.

★ Black Forest Torte

This rich torte is so impressive, thanks to its combination of moist cake layers, chocolate-almond and cream fillings, cherry topping and almond-studded sides. It's almost too pretty to cut! Don't hesitate, though—no one will be able to resist a slice, no matter how stuffed they are. ~Doris Grotz, York, Nebraska

2/3 cup butter, softened
1-3/4 cups sugar
4 eggs
1-1/4 cups water
4 squares (1 ounce *each*) unsweetened chocolate
1 teaspoon vanilla extract
1-3/4 cups all-purpose flour
1 teaspoon baking powder
1/4 teaspoon baking soda
CHOCOLATE FILLING:
6 ounces German sweet chocolate
3/4 cup butter, cubed
1/2 cup sliced almonds, toasted
CREAM FILLING:
3 cups heavy whipping cream
2 tablespoons sugar
2 teaspoons vanilla extract
TOPPING:
1 cup cherry pie filling
3 cups sliced almonds, toasted

1. In a large mixing bowl, cream butter and sugar. Add eggs, one at a time, beating well after each addition. Beat in water just until blended. In a microwave-safe bowl, melt chocolate; stir in vanilla until smooth. Combine the flour, baking powder and baking soda; add to creamed mixture alternately with chocolate mixture. Beat until smooth.

2. Pour into four greased and floured 9-in. round baking pans. Bake at 350° for 15-20 minutes or until a toothpick inserted near the center comes out clean. Cool for 10 minutes before removing from pans to wire racks to cool completely.

3. For chocolate filling, in a microwave-safe bowl, melt chocolate. Stir in butter until smooth and melted. Add almonds.

4. For cream filling, in a small mixing bowl, beat cream until it begins to thicken. Add sugar and vanilla; beat until soft peaks form.

5. To assemble, place one cake on a serving platter; spread with a fourth of the chocolate filling and a fourth of the cream filling. Repeat layers twice. Top with remaining cake and chocolate filling.

6. Place 1-1/2 cups of the remaining cream filling in a pastry bag with a large star pastry tip. Pipe around edge of cake. Fill center with cherry pie filling. Spread remaining cream filling over sides of cake; press almonds into sides. Store in the refrigerator. **Yield:** 16 servings.

★ French Cream with Sugared Grapes

Looking for a truly elegant finale for your holiday dinner? My dessert will do the trick. It looks so regal surrounded by pretty sugared fruit, and the flavor is divine. A friend gave me this recipe several years ago, and it's been in high demand at my house ever since. ~June Bridges, Franklin, Indiana

1 cup (8 ounces) sour cream
1 cup heavy whipping cream
3/4 cup sugar
1 envelope unflavored gelatin
1/4 cup cold water
1 package (8 ounces) cream cheese, softened
1 teaspoon vanilla extract
Seedless green and red grapes
Additional sugar

1. In a saucepan, combine sour cream and cream until well blended. Gradually stir in sugar. Cook and stir over medium heat just until mixture is warm and sugar is dissolved. Remove from the heat.

2. In a small microwave-safe bowl, sprinkle gelatin over cold water; let stand for 1 minute. Microwave, uncovered, on high for 40 seconds. Stir; let stand for 1 minute or until gelatin is completely dissolved. Stir into sour cream mixture.

3. In a small mixing bowl, beat cream cheese until light and fluffy. Gradually add gelatin cream mixture and vanilla, beating on low speed until combined. Pour into a 4-cup mold coated with nonstick cooking spray. Chill for at least 4 hours or until set.

4. Dip grapes into water and shake off excess moisture; dip into sugar, turning to coat. Unmold dessert onto a serving plat-

Black Forest Torte

Lemon Pepper Biscotti (p. 56)
Mild Tomato Salsa (p. 56)
Chocolaty Popcorn

Gifts of Good Taste

★ Chocolaty Popcorn

Pack this irresistible snack into wax or plastic bags and tie them shut with curling ribbons for a pretty presentation. You could also prepare a batch or two for a holiday bake sale. I guarantee it'll go quickly! ~Diane Halferty, Corpus Christi, Texas

- 12 cups butter-flavored microwave popcorn
- 1 package (12 ounces) semisweet chocolate chips
- 2 teaspoons shortening, *divided*
- 1 package (10 to 12 ounces) vanilla *or* white chips
- 2 cups coarsely chopped pecans, toasted

1. Place the popcorn in a greased 15-in. x 10-in. x 1-in. pan; set aside. Place semisweet chocolate chips and 1 teaspoon shortening in a microwave-safe bowl. Microwave, uncovered, at 70% power for 1 minute; stir until smooth. Drizzle over popcorn.

2. Place vanilla chips and remaining shortening in a microwave-safe bowl. Microwave, uncovered, at 70% power for 1 minute; stir until smooth. Drizzle over popcorn; toss gently to coat as much popcorn as possible. Sprinkle with pecans. Chill until firm before breaking into pieces. **Yield:** 16 cups.

Editor's Note: This recipe was tested in a 1,100-watt microwave.

Pistachio Butter

This spread is easy, elegant and yummy. I like to scoop portions into small yet sturdy foil pans, cover them with clear plastic wrap and add a cheery ribbon before handing out this present to friends. ~Marilyn Houghton Kayton, Naperville, Illinois

- 1 cup butter, softened
- 1/4 cup honey
- 1 tablespoon peach *or* apricot gelatin powder
- 1/4 cup chopped pistachios

In a small mixing bowl, beat the butter, honey and gelatin powder until smooth. Stir in pistachios. Transfer to small airtight containers. Cover and refrigerate for up to 1 month. **Yield:** 1-1/2 cups.

★ Spice Mix for Chili

This spice mix comes from my mother's chili recipe, which is fantastic. It'll make a great gift for the hearty eaters you know, especially if you pair it with a loaf of bread.
~Vivian Huizinga, Shallow Lake, Ontario

- 3-1/2 teaspoons garlic salt
- 3-1/2 teaspoons chili powder
- 2 teaspoons *each* salt, onion powder, pepper, ground cumin, paprika and dried parsley flakes
- 1/2 teaspoon cayenne pepper

ADDITIONAL INGREDIENTS (for *each* batch):
- 1 pound ground beef
- 1 medium onion, chopped
- 1 cup sliced fresh mushrooms, optional
- 1 can (28 ounces) diced tomatoes, undrained
- 1 can (16 ounces) kidney beans, rinsed and drained
- 1 can (15-1/2 ounces) hot chili beans, undrained
- 1 can (10-3/4 ounces) condensed tomato soup, undiluted
- 1 teaspoon Worcestershire sauce
- 2 garlic cloves, minced

Shredded cheddar cheese

1. In a small bowl, combine all of the seasonings; mix well. Store in an airtight container in a cool dry place for up to 6 months. **Yield:** 3 batches (about 6 tablespoons total).

2. To prepare chili: In a large saucepan or Dutch oven, cook the beef, onion and mushrooms if desired over medium heat until meat is no longer pink; drain.

3. Stir in the tomatoes, beans, soup, 2 tablespoons spice mix, Worcestershire sauce and garlic. Bring to a boil. Reduce heat; cover and simmer for 20 minutes, stirring occasionally. Garnish with cheese. **Yield:** 8-10 servings.

Spice Mix for Chili

Peanut Butter Brownie Mix

★ Mild Tomato Salsa

(Pictured on page 54)

I got this salsa recipe from my sister, and my children and I have been making batches of it ever since. We pair pint jars with packages of tortilla chips for zesty Christmas gifts. When the kids give this present to their teachers, they can truly say they helped make it. ~Pamela Lundstrom, Bird Island, Minnesota

    36 medium tomatoes, peeled and quartered
     4 medium green peppers, chopped
     3 large onions, chopped
     2 cans (12 ounces *each*) tomato paste
 1-3/4 cups white vinegar
   1/2 cup sugar
     1 medium sweet red pepper, chopped
     1 celery rib, chopped
    15 garlic cloves, minced
     4 to 5 jalapeno peppers, seeded and chopped
   1/4 cup canning salt
   1/4 to 1/2 teaspoon hot pepper sauce

1. In a large kettle, cook tomatoes, uncovered, over medium heat for 20 minutes. Drain, reserving 2 cups liquid. Return tomatoes to the kettle.

2. Stir in the green peppers, onions, tomato paste, vinegar, sugar, red pepper, celery, garlic, jalapenos, canning salt, hot pepper sauce and reserved tomato liquid. Bring to a boil. Reduce heat; simmer, uncovered, for 1 hour, stirring frequently.

3. Ladle hot mixture into hot jars, leaving 1/4-in. headspace. Adjust caps. Process for 20 minutes in a boiling-water bath. **Yield:** 10 pints.

Editor's Note: When cutting or seeding hot peppers, use rubber or plastic gloves to protect your hands. Avoid touching your face.

★ Peanut Butter Brownie Mix

I discovered this recipe in our local newspaper, gave it a try, and my family loved it. If you pack the dry ingredients in a quart canning jar, you can cover the lid with Christmasy fabric for a quick, festive touch. ~Lynn Dowdall, Perth, Ontario

     1 cup packed brown sugar
   1/2 cup sugar
   1/3 cup baking cocoa
     1 cup peanut butter chips
     1 cup all-purpose flour
   1/2 teaspoon baking powder
   1/4 teaspoon salt
   1/2 cup semisweet chocolate chips
   1/2 cup chopped walnuts
ADDITIONAL INGREDIENTS:
     2 eggs
   1/2 cup butter, melted
     1 teaspoon vanilla extract

1. In a 1-qt. glass container, layer the first nine ingredients in order listed, packing well between each layer. Cover tightly. Store in a cool dry place for up to 6 months.

2. To prepare brownies: In a bowl, combine the eggs, butter, vanilla and brownie mix. Spread into a greased 8-in. square baking dish. Bake at 350° for 25-30 minutes or until set (do not overbake). Cool on a wire rack. Cut into squares. **Yield:** 16 brownies.

★ Lemon Pepper Biscotti

(Pictured on page 54)

Flavored with a zesty combination of black pepper, garlic, lemon and Parmesan cheese, these crisp, savory "cookies"—a fun variation on the sweet version—are great for dipping or solo snacking. ~Dorothy Smith, El Dorado, Arkansas

   1/2 cup butter, softened
     2 tablespoons sugar
     1 garlic clove, minced
     2 eggs
 2-1/4 cups all-purpose flour
   1/2 cup grated Parmesan cheese
     2 tablespoons minced fresh parsley
     4 teaspoons grated lemon peel
 1-1/2 teaspoons baking powder
     1 to 2 teaspoons coarsely ground pepper
   1/2 teaspoon salt

1. In a large mixing bowl, cream the butter, sugar and garlic until fluffy. Add eggs, one at a time, beating well after each addition. Combine the flour, Parmesan cheese, parsley, lemon peel, baking powder, pepper and salt; gradually add to creamed mixture, beating until blended (dough will be stiff).

2. Divide dough in half. On an ungreased baking sheet, roll each portion into a 12-in. log. Bake at 350° for 25-30 minutes or until golden brown. Carefully transfer to a wire rack; cool for 15 minutes.

3. Transfer to a cutting board; cut diagonally with a sharp knife into 1/2-in. slices. Place cut side down on ungreased baking sheets. Bake for 10 minutes. Turn; bake 10 minutes longer or until lightly browned and firm. Remove to wire racks to cool. Store in an airtight container. **Yield:** 2 dozen.

Sugared Citrus Walnuts

These sweet nuts are great at a holiday party or to give as a gift. People just can't stop snacking on them once they've started. My grandmother encouraged me to try new things in the kitchen when I was young, and I still do that today. I hope my son will follow in his mother's and great-grandmother's culinary footsteps!
~Samantha Jones, Morgantown, West Virginia

   2 cups sugar
1/4 cup water
1/4 cup orange juice
1/4 cup grated lemon peel
1/4 cup grated orange peel
   3 cups walnut halves

1. Line a 15-in. x 10-in. x 1-in. baking pan with foil and butter the foil; set aside. In a heavy saucepan, combine the sugar, water and orange juice. Cook and stir over medium heat until a candy thermometer reads 244° (firm-ball stage).

2. Remove from the heat; stir in lemon and orange peel. Add walnuts; stir to coat. Transfer to prepared pan. Cool, stirring several times. **Yield:** about 5 cups.

Editor's Note: We recommend that you test your candy thermometer before each use by bringing water to a boil; the thermometer should read 212°. Adjust your recipe temperature up or down based on your test.

Pumpkin Banana Bread

I came across this recipe about 10 years ago, and I still make the bread on a regular basis. The recipe conveniently yields a quartet of mini loaves, making gift-giving easy.
~Linda Wood, Roanoke, Virginia

1/2 cup shortening
1-1/2 cups sugar
   2 eggs
   1 cup mashed ripe bananas (about 2 medium)
3/4 cup canned pumpkin
   1 teaspoon vanilla extract
1-3/4 cups all-purpose flour
1-1/2 teaspoons baking powder
3/4 teaspoon baking soda
1/2 teaspoon salt
1/2 cup chopped walnuts *or* pecans

1. In a large mixing bowl, cream shortening and sugar. Add eggs, one at a time, beating well after each addition. Beat in bananas, pumpkin and vanilla. Combine the flour, baking powder, baking soda and salt; gradually add to creamed mixture. Fold in nuts.

2. Pour into four greased 5-3/4-in. x 3-in. x 2-in. loaf pans. Bake at 350° for 35-40 minutes or until a toothpick inserted near the center comes out clean. Cool for 10 minutes before removing from pans to wire racks. **Yield:** 4 mini loaves.

★ Little Holiday Cakes

This recipe came from a college friend some 25 years ago. People are surprised to find jam sandwiched between the flaky pie crust and sweet cake topped with frosting. The combination is a real winner.   *~Dana Beckstrom, Salt Lake City, Utah*

Pastry for double-crust pie (9 inches)
   1/2 cup seedless raspberry jam
     1 package (18-1/4 ounces) red velvet cake mix
     1 can (16 ounces) vanilla frosting
Red and green sprinkles

1. Roll pastry to 1/8-in. thickness. Cut into 2-1/2-in. circles. Press onto the bottom and 1/2 in. up the sides of greased muffin cups. Top each with 1 teaspoon of jam; set aside.

2. Prepare cake batter according to package directions; fill muffin cups three-fourths full. Bake at 350° for 14-16 minutes or until a toothpick comes out clean. Cool for 10 minutes before removing from pans to wire racks to cool completely. Frost with vanilla frosting and decorate with sprinkles. **Yield:** 2 dozen.

Little Holiday Cakes

Lemon Poppy Seed Cookies (p. 60)
Poinsettia Cookies
Cranberry Rugalach (p. 61)

Christmas Cookie Parade

★ Poinsettia Cookies

To make these, I adapted a traditional cherry blossom cookie recipe by leaving out the lemon zest and adding food coloring, sprinkles and almond extract to create a more festive look and flavor. When I took a batch to a cookie exchange party, everyone raved about them. ~Gloria Ward, Mesa, Arizona

1/2 cup butter, softened
1/2 cup sugar
1 egg
1 tablespoon milk
1/2 teaspoon almond extract
1/2 teaspoon cherry *or* vanilla extract
4 to 5 drops red food coloring, optional
1-3/4 cups all-purpose flour
1 teaspoon baking powder
1/4 teaspoon salt
1/2 cup candied cherry halves
Pink *or* red sprinkles, optional

1. In a large mixing bowl, cream butter and sugar. Beat in the egg, milk, extracts and food coloring if desired. Combine the flour, baking powder and salt; gradually add to creamed mixture. Cover and refrigerate for 30 minutes or until easy to handle.

2. Roll dough into 1-1/4-in. balls. Place 2 in. apart on parchment paper-lined baking sheets. With kitchen scissors, snip the top of each ball in half, cutting three-fourths of the way through. Cut each half into thirds; carefully spread the wedges apart, forming flower petals.

3. Place a cherry half in the center of each; top with sprinkles if desired. Bake at 350° for 10-12 minutes or until set. Cool for 1-2 minutes before removing from pans to wire racks. **Yield:** about 3 dozen.

Pecan Crescents

This recipe came from a church cookbook. I altered a few ingredients, and everyone who tries these crescents likes the nice, nutty flavor and texture. ~Kathy Henson, Alice, Texas

1 cup butter, softened
3/4 cup sugar
1-1/2 teaspoons almond extract
2-1/2 cups all-purpose flour
1 cup ground pecans
1 cup confectioners' sugar

1. In a large mixing bowl, cream butter and sugar. Beat in extract. Gradually add flour. Stir in the pecans.

2. Shape teaspoonfuls of dough into crescents. Place 2 in. apart on ungreased baking sheets. Bake at 300° for 18-20 minutes or until firm. Roll warm cookies in confectioners' sugar. Cool on wire racks. **Yield:** 9 dozen.

★ Brazil Nut Cookies

Brazil nuts may be an unusual ingredient for cookies, but the flavor is outstanding. ~Charlotte Mains, Cuyahoga Falls, Ohio

1 cup butter, softened
1 cup sugar
2 eggs
1-1/2 teaspoons vanilla extract
2-1/4 cups all-purpose flour
1/2 teaspoon baking soda
1/4 teaspoon salt
2 cups chopped Brazil nuts
1/2 cup flaked coconut

1. In a large mixing bowl, cream butter and sugar. Add eggs, one at a time, beating well after each addition. Beat in vanilla. Combine the flour, baking soda and salt; gradually add to creamed mixture. Stir in nuts and coconut.

2. Drop by tablespoonfuls 3 in. apart onto ungreased baking sheets. Bake at 350° for 10-12 minutes or until bottom of cookies are lightly browned. Remove to wire racks. **Yield:** about 4-1/2 dozen.

Brazil Nut Cookies

Chocolate-Dipped Orange Cookies

★ Chocolate-Dipped Orange Cookies

These tender cookies are pretty to look at—and the combination of cream cheese, orange, chocolate and almonds makes them almost irresistible. ~Linda Call, Falun, Kansas

    1 cup butter, softened
    1 package (8 ounces) cream cheese, softened
    1 cup sugar
    1/2 teaspoon vanilla extract
    2 tablespoons grated orange peel
2-1/2 cups all-purpose flour
    1/2 teaspoon salt
    1 cup finely chopped blanched almonds
GLAZE:
    5 squares (1 ounce *each*) semisweet chocolate
    3 tablespoons butter
    1/4 cup finely chopped blanched almonds

1. In a large mixing bowl, cream the butter, cream cheese and sugar. Beat in vanilla and orange peel. Combine the flour and salt; gradually add to creamed mixture. Stir in almonds.

2. Roll into 1-in. balls. Place 2 in. apart on ungreased baking sheets. Flatten with a glass dipped in sugar. Bake at 325° for 20-25 minutes or until firm. Remove to wire racks to cool.

3. For glaze, in a microwave-safe bowl, melt chocolate and butter; stir until smooth. Dip each cookie halfway into chocolate; shake off excess. Immediately sprinkle with almonds. Place on waxed paper to harden. **Yield:** 6 dozen.

★ Lemon Poppy Seed Cookies

(Pictured on page 58)

These soft cookies are definitely a comforting old-fashioned variety everyone will enjoy. ~Pat Woolley, Jackson Center, Ohio

    1/2 cup poppy seed filling
    2 teaspoons lemon juice
    1 cup butter, softened
1-1/2 cups sugar
    3 egg yolks
    1 tablespoon grated lemon peel
    2 teaspoons lemon extract
    1 teaspoon vanilla extract
3-1/2 cups all-purpose flour
    2 teaspoons baking powder
1-1/4 teaspoons baking soda
    3/4 cup buttermilk
FROSTING:
    3 cups confectioners' sugar
    2 tablespoons butter, softened
    1/4 cup milk
    2 teaspoons lemon extract
    1 teaspoon grated lemon peel
Poppy seeds, optional

1. In a small bowl, combine the poppy seed filling and lemon juice; set aside. In a large mixing bowl, cream the butter and sugar. Beat in the egg yolks, lemon peel and extracts. Combine the flour, baking powder and baking soda; add to creamed mixture alternately with buttermilk.

2. Drop by tablespoonfuls onto greased baking sheets. Using the end of a wooden spoon handle, make an indentation about 1/2 in. deep in the center of each. Fill with about 1/2 teaspoon of poppy seed filling. Top with a teaspoonful of dough. Bake at 350° for 14-16 minutes or until edges are golden brown. Remove to wire racks to cool.

3. For frosting, in a small mixing bowl, beat the confectioners' sugar, butter, milk, extract and lemon peel until smooth. Spread over cookies. Sprinkle with poppy seeds if desired. **Yield:** 3-1/2 dozen.

Almond-Cherry Cake Brownies

After I purchased a huge jar of cherries at an outlet store, I realized I needed more recipe ideas for them. I started experimenting and came up with these fudgy bars. Happily, my family loves them! ~Trudy Holmen, North Bend, Oregon

    1/2 cup butter, softened
    1 cup sugar
    3 eggs
    2 teaspoons almond extract
1-1/4 cups chocolate syrup
1-1/4 cups all-purpose flour
    1 jar (10 ounces) maraschino cherries, drained and chopped
    3/4 cup flaked coconut
    1/2 cup chopped slivered almonds
FROSTING:
    1/4 cup butter
    1/4 cup baking cocoa
1-1/2 cups confectioners' sugar
    1/4 teaspoon almond extract
    3 to 4 tablespoons milk

1. In a large mixing bowl, cream butter and sugar. Beat in eggs and extract. Add chocolate syrup and flour; mix well. Stir in cherries, coconut and almonds.

2. Pour into a greased 13-in. x 9-in. x 2-in. baking pan. Bake at 350° for 35-40 minutes or until a toothpick inserted near the center comes out clean and edges pull away from sides of pan. Cool on a wire rack.

3. For frosting, in a saucepan, combine butter and cocoa. Cook and stir until butter is melted and mixture is smooth. Remove from the heat. Whisk in confectioners' sugar and extract. Add enough milk to achieve desired consistency. Spread over brownies. **Yield:** 3 dozen.

★ Cranberry Rugalach

(Pictured on page 58)

These traditional Polish treats will keep for a long time in an airtight container. One Christmas, I sent a batch to my sister, but the box got lost. She received it 12 days later...and the cookies still tasted great! ~Jean Doxon, Omaha, Nebraska

    1 cup butter, softened
    1 package (8 ounces) cream cheese, softened
  1/2 cup sugar
2-3/4 cups all-purpose flour
    1 teaspoon salt
FILLING:
  3/4 cup sugar
  2/3 cup dried cranberries, finely chopped
  1/2 cup finely chopped walnuts, toasted
  1/3 cup butter, melted
    2 teaspoons ground cinnamon
    1 teaspoon ground allspice
    1 egg, beaten
Additional sugar

1. In a large mixing bowl, cream the butter, cream cheese and sugar. Gradually add flour and salt. Turn onto a lightly floured surface; knead for 3 minutes or until smooth. Divide into eight portions. Roll each portion into a ball; flatten into a 4-in. circle. Wrap in plastic wrap and refrigerate for at least 1 hour.

2. In a bowl, combine the sugar, cranberries, walnuts, butter, cinnamon and allspice. On a lightly floured surface, roll one portion of dough into an 8-in. circle. Sprinkle with 3 tablespoons of filling to within 1/2 in. of edges. Cut into eight wedges.

3. Roll up wedges from the wide end and place point side down 2 in. apart on foil-lined baking sheets. Curve ends down to form a crescent shape. Brush with egg and sprinkle with sugar.

4. Repeat with remaining dough and filling. Bake at 350° for 18-20 minutes or until golden brown. Remove to wire racks. **Yield:** about 5 dozen.

★ Candied Orange Date Bars

A good friend of mine gave me the recipe for these yummy, rich date bars. Chopped candied orange slices really make them special. I dip my kitchen shears in hot water to make cutting the orange slices a little easier. ~Eunice Stoen, Decorah, Iowa

    1 package (7 ounces) orange candy slices
  1/2 cup sugar
    2 tablespoons plus 1-3/4 cups all-purpose flour, *divided*
  1/2 cup water
  1/2 pound chopped dates
    1 cup butter, softened
    1 cup packed brown sugar
    2 eggs
    1 teaspoon baking soda
  1/2 teaspoon salt
  1/2 cup chopped walnuts
Confectioners' sugar

1. Cut orange slices horizontally in half, then into 1/4-in. pieces; set aside. In a saucepan, combine the sugar and 2 tablespoons flour. Stir in water until smooth. Add dates. Bring to a boil; cook and stir for 2 minutes or until thickened. Remove from the heat; cool.

2. In a large mixing bowl, cream butter and brown sugar. Add eggs, one at a time, beating well after each addition. Combine the baking soda, salt and remaining flour; add to creamed mixture. Stir in walnuts.

3. Spread half of the batter into a greased 13-in. x 9-in. x 2-in. baking pan. Spread date mixture over batter; sprinkle with reserved orange pieces. Spread remaining batter over the top. Bake at 350° for 30-35 minutes or until a toothpick inserted near the center comes out clean. Cool on a wire rack. Dust with confectioners' sugar. **Yield:** about 3 dozen.

    Editor's Note: To make cutting orange slices easier, use a kitchen shears dipped in water. Or, first toss them in 1 to 2 tablespoons confectioners' sugar; use a mesh strainer or colander to shake off excess sugar.

Candied Orange Date Bars

Chewy Fruit Cookies

★ Chewy Fruit Cookies

This recipe, given to me by a friend years ago, was one I used to save just for Christmas. But friends and family began to request them regularly, and now I buy extra candied cherries when they go on sale in December so I can make the treats all year long.
~Barbara Burrow, Thompsons Station, Tennessee

   1/2 cup shortening
     1 cup packed brown sugar
     1 egg
   1/4 cup buttermilk
1-3/4 cups all-purpose flour
   1/2 teaspoon salt
   1/2 teaspoon baking soda
     1 cup halved candied cherries
     1 cup chopped dates
   3/4 cup chopped pecans
    36 pecan halves

1. In a small mixing bowl, cream shortening and brown sugar. Add egg and buttermilk; mix well. Combine the flour, salt and baking soda; gradually add to creamed mixture. Stir in the cherries, dates and chopped pecans.

2. Drop by heaping tablespoonfuls 2 in. apart onto lightly greased baking sheets. Top each with a pecan half. Bake at 350° for 12-15 minutes or until golden brown. Remove to wire racks. **Yield:** 3 dozen.

★ Lemon Ginger Cutouts

I like to bake these cutouts for Thanksgiving and Christmas, then decorate them in the colors of the season. If I run out of time before the holidays, I simply skip the frosting step and sprinkle the colored sugar directly on the cookies before they go in the oven. The end result is just as festive and still yummy.
~Victoria Sampson, Hendersonville, North Carolina

     1 cup butter, softened
   2/3 cup packed brown sugar
   2/3 cup light corn syrup
   1/3 cup honey

     1 teaspoon grated lemon peel
4-1/2 cups all-purpose flour
     1 teaspoon salt
     1 teaspoon baking soda
     1 teaspoon ground cinnamon
   3/4 teaspoon ground ginger
FROSTING:
1-1/2 cups confectioners' sugar
     1 to 2 tablespoons water
Colored sugar, optional

1. In a large mixing bowl, cream butter and brown sugar. Gradually add corn syrup, honey and lemon peel. Combine the flour, salt, baking soda, cinnamon and ginger; gradually add to creamed mixture and mix well. Cover and refrigerate for 2 hours or until easy to handle.

2. Divide dough into fourths. On a lightly floured surface, roll one portion to 1/8-in. thickness. Cut into desired shapes with floured 2-in. cookie cutters. Place 2 in. apart on greased baking sheets. Bake at 350° for 8-10 minutes or until light golden brown. Remove to wire racks to cool. Repeat with remaining dough.

3. For frosting, in a small bowl, combine confectioners' sugar and enough water to achieve desired consistency. Spread over cookies. Sprinkle with colored sugar if desired. **Yield:** about 8 dozen.

Pine Nut Thumbprints

Want to try a variation on the classic thumbprint cookie? Give my recipe a try. I use pine nuts, orange juice and marmalade to create a crunchy, citrusy holiday cookie that everyone likes.
~Iola Egle, Bella Vista, Arkansas

   1/2 cup butter, softened
   1/4 cup packed brown sugar
     1 egg yolk
     1 teaspoon grated lemon peel
     1 teaspoon vanilla extract
     1 cup all-purpose flour
   1/4 teaspoon salt
     2 tablespoons honey
     1 tablespoon orange juice
   3/4 cup finely chopped pine nuts
   1/4 cup orange marmalade

1. In a small mixing bowl, cream butter and brown sugar. Beat in egg yolk, lemon peel and vanilla. Combine the flour and salt; gradually add to creamed mixture. Cover and refrigerate for 1 hour or until easy to handle.

2. Roll the dough into 1-in. balls. In a shallow bowl, combine honey and orange juice. Dip the balls into honey mixture, then roll in chopped pine nuts. Place 1 in. apart on greased baking sheets.

3. Using the end of a wooden spoon handle, make an indentation in the center of each ball. Bake at 350° for 10-12 minutes or until edges are lightly browned. Remove to wire racks. Fill centers with marmalade; cool completely. **Yield:** 2 dozen.

Lemon Ginger Cutouts

Peanut Butter Snowballs (p. 66)
Chocolate Peppermint Bark
Nutty Caramels

Sweet Indulgences

✯ Nutty Caramels

A cousin passed this quick and easy recipe on to me. We make it every Christmas and include the caramels in gift baskets we share with family and friends. ~*Lynn Nelson, Kasilof, Alaska*

> 1 teaspoon butter plus 1/4 cup butter, *divided*
> 1 cup sugar
> 1 cup light corn syrup
> 1 cup evaporated milk
> 1 cup chopped nuts
> 1 teaspoon vanilla extract

1. Line a 9-in. square pan with foil and grease the foil with 1 teaspoon butter; set aside. In a heavy saucepan, combine the sugar, corn syrup, milk and remaining butter. Cook and stir over medium heat until sugar is dissolved. Bring to a rapid boil, stirring constantly, until a candy thermometer reads 248° (firm-ball stage).

2. Remove from the heat; stir in nuts and vanilla. Pour into prepared pan (do not scrape saucepan). Cool completely. Using foil, lift caramels out of pan; discard foil. Cut into 1-in. squares. **Yield:** 1-1/2 pounds.

Editor's Note: We recommend that you test your candy thermometer before each use by bringing water to a boil; the thermometer should read 212°. Adjust your recipe temperature up or down based on your test.

✯ Chocolate Peppermint Bark

These candies are such a snap to make, I almost feel guilty serving them...but the chocolate and mint flavors always bring guests back for more! ~*Keslie Beck Houser, Pasco, Washington*

> 6 squares (1 ounce *each*) white baking chocolate
> 1 cup (6 ounces) semisweet chocolate chips
> 1 cup crushed peppermint candies, *divided*

1. In a microwave-safe bowl, melt white chocolate at 70% power; stir until smooth. Repeat with chocolate chips. Stir 6 tablespoons of crushed peppermint candies into each bowl. Drop white chocolate and semisweet chocolate in alternating spoonfuls onto a waxed paper-lined baking sheet.

2. With a metal spatula, cut through chocolate to swirl, spreading to 1/4-in. thickness. Sprinkle with remaining crushed candies. Chill until firm. Break into pieces. Store in an airtight container in the refrigerator. **Yield:** about 1 pound.

Editor's Note: This recipe was tested in a 1,100-watt microwave.

✯ Coconut Chocolate-Covered Cherries

A friend gave me this recipe because she knew how much I like chocolate-covered cherries. Coconut and nuts make this version absolutely divine. ~*Sylvia Chiappone, San Ardo, California*

> 1/2 cup butter, softened
> 3-3/4 cups confectioners' sugar
> 1/2 cup sweetened condensed milk
> 1 teaspoon vanilla extract
> 2 cups flaked coconut
> 2 cups finely chopped walnuts
> 2 jars (16 ounces *each*) maraschino cherries with stems, well drained and patted dry
> 2 packages (11-1/2 ounces *each*) milk chocolate chips
> 1 tablespoon shortening

1. In a large mixing bowl, beat butter and confectioners' sugar until smooth. Beat in milk and vanilla until well blended and mixture looks like softened butter. Fold in the coconut and walnuts.

2. With moist hands, shape 2 teaspoonfuls of coconut mixture around each cherry, forming a ball. Place on a waxed paper-lined baking sheet. Cover and refrigerate for 1 hour or until chilled.

3. In a microwave-safe bowl, melt chocolate chips and shortening; stir until smooth. Dip coated cherries into chocolate. Place on waxed paper; let stand until set. Store in an airtight container at room temperature for up to 1 month. **Yield:** about 5 dozen.

Coconut Chocolate-Covered Cherries

Mixed Nut-Cornflake Brittle

★ Mixed Nut-Cornflake Brittle

This five-ingredient brittle is one of the best I've ever made. The recipe is so easy to follow and can be completed in about 30 minutes. Friends ask me for the recipe all the time.
~Rosemary Lorentz, Stratford, Ontario

```
  3/4 cup sugar
  1/2 cup light corn syrup
  1/4 cup butter
    6 cups cornflakes
1-1/2 cups mixed nuts
```

1. Line a 15-in. x 10-in. x 1-in. baking pan with foil and heavily grease the foil; set aside. In a large heavy saucepan, combine the sugar, corn syrup and butter. Cook and stir over medium-high heat until sugar is dissolved and mixture begins to boil. Remove from the heat. Stir in cornflakes and nuts.

2. Spread into prepared pan. Bake at 300° for 25 minutes. Cool on a wire rack. Break into pieces. Store at room temperature in an airtight container. **Yield:** about 1-1/4 pounds.

★ Peanut Butter Snowballs

(Pictured on page 64)

I like to make these coconut-covered balls when the snow is flying outside. I've shared the candies with many of my friends and family members, and everyone loves them.
~Lucille Johnson, Vale, North Carolina

```
2 cups nonfat dry milk powder
1 cup chunky peanut butter
1 cup honey
1 teaspoon vanilla extract
8 ounces white candy coating, coarsely chopped
```

1/4 cup shortening
3 cups flaked coconut

1. In a large mixing bowl, combine the milk powder, peanut butter, honey and vanilla. Shape into 1-in. balls. Place on a waxed paper-lined baking sheet. Let stand, uncovered, for 30 minutes.

2. In a microwave-safe bowl, melt candy coating and shortening at 70% power for 1-2 minutes; stir until smooth. Dip balls into coating, then roll in coconut. Return to baking sheet; let stand until set. Store in an airtight container at room temperature. **Yield:** 3 dozen.

Editor's Note: This recipe was tested in a 1,100-watt microwave.

Sour Cream Walnut Fudge

This white fudge is my all-time favorite. I first tried it on my birthday and had to request the recipe. To speed up the 8-minute beating time, I recruit "kitchen helpers" who take turns stirring the mixture—with the promise that they'll get some of the treats!
~Virginia Facemeyer, Mount Vernon, Ohio

```
1 teaspoon plus 2 tablespoons butter, divided
2 cups sugar
1/2 cup sour cream
1/3 cup light corn syrup
1/4 teaspoon salt
2 teaspoons vanilla extract
1 cup chopped walnuts
```

1. Line an 8-in. square pan with foil and grease the foil with 1 teaspoon butter; set aside. In a heavy saucepan, combine the sugar, sour cream, corn syrup, salt and remaining butter. Bring to a boil over medium heat; cook until a candy thermometer reads 238° (soft-ball stage).

2. Remove from the heat; stir in vanilla. Let stand, without stirring, for 15 minutes. Add walnuts. With a wooden spoon, beat until thick and creamy, about 8 minutes. Pour into prepared pan. Refrigerate until firm.

3. Using foil, lift fudge out of pan. Discard foil; cut fudge into 1-in. squares. Store in an airtight container in the refrigerator. **Yield:** about 1-1/2 pounds.

Editor's Note: We recommend that you test your candy thermometer before each use by bringing water to a boil; the thermometer should read 212°. Adjust your recipe temperature up or down based on your test.

Butterscotch Fudge

Friends often ask my daughter to talk me into making some of this fudge—everyone really enjoys it. The butterscotch flavor is rich and different. ~Iris Nelson, Leaf Rapids, Manitoba

```
1 teaspoon plus 1/2 cup butter, divided
2 cups sugar
1 cup evaporated milk
```

1 package (10 to 11 ounces) butterscotch chips
1-1/2 cups graham cracker crumbs

1. Line an 8-in. square pan with foil and grease the foil with 1 teaspoon butter; set aside. In a small heavy saucepan, combine the sugar, milk and remaining butter. Bring to a boil; cook for 5 minutes. Remove from the heat. Add butterscotch chips and graham cracker crumbs; stir until chips are melted.

2. Pour into prepared pan. Refrigerate until firm. Using foil, lift fudge out of pan. Discard foil; cut fudge into 1-in. squares. Store in an airtight container in the refrigerator. **Yield:** 2-1/2 pounds.

Tart 'n' Sweet Grapefruit Peel

I hadn't made this recipe for some 20 years...then I spotted something in a magazine that made me think of it. The candied peel was so tasty, I don't think I'll put the recipe away again!
~Anna Levy, Coopersburg, Pennsylvania

   2 large grapefruit
2-1/2 cups sugar, *divided*
1-3/4 cups water
  1/2 cup honey
  1/4 teaspoon salt

1. With a sharp knife, score each grapefruit into four wedge-shaped sections. Loosen and remove peel with a spoon (save fruit for another use). Place peel in a heavy saucepan and cover with cold water; bring to a boil. Reduce heat; cover and simmer for 30 minutes. Drain. Repeat process twice, draining each time. Cool for 5 minutes. Carefully scrape excess pulp from peel. Cut into 1/4-in. strips.

2. In another saucepan, combine 1-1/2 cups sugar, water, honey and salt. Cook over medium heat until sugar is dissolved. Add grapefruit strips; boil gently for 50-60 minutes or until almost all of the syrup is absorbed and peel is transparent, stirring occasionally (watch carefully to prevent scorching).

3. Drain strips in a colander; let stand for 10 minutes. Sprinkle remaining sugar into an ungreased 15-in. x 10-in. x 1-in. baking pan. Sprinkle strips over sugar; toss to coat. Let stand for 8 hours or overnight, tossing occasionally. Store in an airtight container for up to 3 weeks. **Yield:** about 3 cups.

Peanut Pretzel Clusters

These fast and delicious morsels will look attractive on a candy-filled tray, and they make great gifts, too. The combination of salty and sweet flavors is one everybody enjoys.
~Stella Champagne, Longwood, Florida

  2 cups vanilla *or* white chips
  1 cup salted peanuts
  1 cup miniature pretzels, broken into small pieces
1/2 cup raisins

In a microwave or heavy saucepan, melt vanilla chips; stir until smooth. Stir in the peanuts, pretzels and raisins. Work-

ing quickly, drop by tablespoonfuls into miniature muffin cup liners. Refrigerate for 1 hour or until firm. Store in an airtight container. **Yield:** 1-1/4 pounds.

★ Pinwheel Mints

Both my grandmother and my mom used to make these eye-catching confections as a replacement for ordinary mints at Christmas. When I offer them at parties, guests tell me the mints are wonderful, and then ask how I created the pretty swirl pattern.   ~Marilou Roth, Milford, Nebraska

  1 package (8 ounces) cream cheese, softened
  1/2 to 1 teaspoon mint extract
7-1/2 to 8-1/2 cups confectioners' sugar
Red and green food coloring
Additional confectioners' sugar

1. In a large mixing bowl, combine cream cheese and mint extract. Gradually beat in as much confectioners' sugar as possible; knead in remaining confectioners' sugar until a firm mixture is achieved. Divide mixture in half; with food coloring, tint half pink and the other light green.

2. On waxed paper, lightly sprinkle remaining confectioners' sugar into a 12-in. x 5-in. rectangle. Divide pink portion in half; shape each portion into a 10-in. log. Place one log on sugared waxed paper and flatten slightly. Cover with waxed paper; roll into a 12-in. x 5-in. rectangle. Repeat with remaining pink portion; set aside. Repeat with light green portion.

3. Remove top piece of waxed paper from one pink and one green rectangle. Place one over the other. Roll up jelly-roll style, starting with a long side. Wrap in waxed paper; twist ends. Repeat. Chill overnight.

4. To serve, cut into 1/2-in. slices. Store in an airtight container in the refrigerator for up to 1 week. **Yield:** about 3 dozen.

Pinwheel Mints

Time to Get Crackin'

This collector turns her home into a nutcracker paradise each Christmas season.

MOST of the year, Joan Solberg's 126-year-old home in Ashland, Wisconsin exudes country elegance and turn-of-the-century grace. But the Christmas season brings about quite a transformation.

"That's when my extensive collection of nutcrackers goes on display and turns the house into a magical dreamland," shares Joan. "My brother, Leon, and I have almost finished refurbishing the historic Victorian home we inherited from our parents, and the nutcrackers fit in perfectly."

Starting in November, she begins to pull out this fes-tive cast of characters, which includes classic soldiers as well as more modern figures such as chefs, sportsmen, Santas, bishops and even the Three Wise Men.

"I love the extra accents that dress up each nutcrack-er and make it so fun to look at. The chefs in particular are so intriguing. They all hold cooking utensils, and sev-eral have trays of treats in their arms," Joan says.

"The chefs brighten my restored kitchen while the other figures top tables, windowsills, bookcases and more throughout the house."

Nutty about Nutcrackers

Joan's standing nutcrackers represent just the outer shell of her collection, however. "I have about 35 actu-al nutcrackers—but anything that has a nutcracker on it is fair game as far as I'm concerned," she says.

"In fact, the very first nutcracker I received wasn't a traditional wooden figure at all. It was a table runner with perfect, tiny nutcrackers cross-stitched on each end. My sister-in-law, Karolyn, made this heirloom for me as a Christmas gift—and I've been bringing home nutcrackers of all kinds ever since."

Joan counts nutcracker-decorated cookie jars, soap dispensers, sheets and pillowcases as part of her collection. "I also have nutcracker-embroidered towels, rugs with nutcrackers, a pretty nutcracker runner in my bedroom, nutcracker soap and a nutcracker teapot. Altogether, I have more than 100 different items featuring my favorite holiday figure," she says.

The 8-foot evergreen she puts up in the living room each year is bedecked with beads, lights and row after row of nutcracker ornaments. "They add so much color and life," she says. "Plus, I have so many that I don't have room for other kinds of tree trims!"

Tasteful Displays

Even Joan's dining room table is touched by nutcrackers. "I have lovely, lace-edged place mats with assorted nutcrackers stitched onto the solid-cloth centers. I pair those with clear glass plates so you can see the stately figures," she says.

"To finish off each place setting, I add a nutcracker coffee cup and a mini nutcracker figurine as a decoration. And when the main meal is over, I like to pull out my favorite dessert plates—trimmed with nutcrackers, of course—and serve festive, homemade cookies and candies. Family and friends compliment me on both my cooking and my collection during dinner parties."

Even before guests ring the doorbell, they're greeted by a lively, giant nutcracker Joan plants in her front yard for the holidays. "It gives them a hint of what they'll find inside," she says. "The clothes I like to wear during the holidays do the same thing—many are embellished with nutcrackers of one sort or another."

Joan's enthusiasm for the sprightly characters spills over into her crafting as well. "I often make holiday mementos by rubber-stamping nutcrackers onto items such as greeting cards and fabric napkins," she says. "I also like to scrapbook, and each Christmas page I create features nutcrackers.

"I don't see a time when I'll tire of these colorful characters. They're so full of holiday cheer that I can't help but add to my collection. Thankfully, our house is spacious. Otherwise, there could come a time when the nutcrackers take over—at least until mid-January, when I tuck them all away until the next Christmas." ▲

ALL KINDS of colorful characters show up in Joan Solberg's home during the holidays. From the Three Wise Men to apron-clad cooks, her Noel nutcrackers appear on place mats, dinnerware, the Christmas tree and more.

Back to Christmas Past

Her timeless creations spell out a connection to days of yore.

ALL THAT GLITTERS in Wendy Addison's romantic holiday creations may not be gold...but the sparkly paper and metal accents she fashions are definitely full of the spirit of yesteryear. That's because this Port Costa, California designer relies on the same simple materials artisans used in the late 1800s to craft ornaments, garlands, tree toppers and other festive delights.

"I've always loved antiques and have been collecting old books, gaslights, kerosene lamps, tinsel, crepe paper and printed materials—such as sheet music, newspaper and greeting cards—for quite a while," Wendy says. "I've also studied art and been actively creating my own drawings and decorations for years. Combining these two passions of mine seems natural.

"When I design, I try to put myself back in time, to imagine what it was like handcrafting Christmas ornaments and everyday decorations 100 years ago. I also use as many vintage materials as I can, including glass glitter made by a German company that's been in business for over a century," she adds.

"Those craftspeople made their own kind of magic using only the simplest of tools and materials, like paper and glitter. I try to follow in their footsteps and do the same thing in the 21st century."

Mixing Old and New

Of course, Wendy's designs do incorporate modern supplies such as cardboard and glue, but vintage items take center stage in all of her work. "I sell many pieces through the Port Costa store I own called Theatre of Dreams, and most of my work revolves around the winter holidays, particularly Christmas," she explains.

Wendy also licenses her designs, but stipulates that as many authentic materials be used in the production as possible. "Nothing's made of plastic," she says with a laugh.

"I've fashioned glitter-covered paper stars of various shapes and sizes, as well as old-fashioned snowflakes. The largest stars and snowflakes can decorate doors or walls, while the smaller versions look pretty when you string them onto garlands or use them to create a mobile...or even sprinkle them on top of the dining table," Wendy relates.

Other decorations include die-cut holiday words and sayings, as well as individual letters, that are all based on similar Victorian-era die-cuts. "These can be used to brighten everything from wreaths to mantels," Wendy says.

"I've also created paper and tinsel candle holders, glittery paper trees, nesting boxes, old-fashioned paper cones that make great tussy mussies and colorful postcard ornaments featuring pictures very much like old-fashioned postcards."

VINTAGE STYLES and craftsmanship inspire Wendy Addison's shiny Christmastime designs, including Victorian-style die-cut words and stars.

Measure of Success

Many of these trims brighten Wendy's Victorian home during the holidays and beyond. "My house and my shop, which is right next door, are my laboratories for trying out decorations," she says.

"Once each piece is completed in my studio, I display it, as much to see how it looks as to gauge people's reactions. If an ornament or garland elicits 'oohs' and 'aahs' from my 18-year-old daughter, Monica, a fellow artist, our friends and my customers, I know I have a winner on my hands."

Attempting to tap into the magic of a bygone era is satisfying for Wendy. "I love the simplicity of the materials and how easily they come together to create a rich, warm look," she says. "Being able to share this enchantment with others is icing on the cake."

Editor's Note: Wendy's old-fashioned designs are available at retail stores nationwide. Contact Midwest/Seasons of Cannon Falls, 32057-64th Ave., Cannon Falls MN 55006, or check the Web site, *www.seasonsofcannon falls.com*, for stores near you. Wendy's shop, Theatre of Dreams, is located at 11 Canyon Lake Dr., Port Costa CA 94569. ▲

Seasonal Crafts

Create your own Christmas magic this season with the exciting holiday projects in this chapter. You'll soon have extra-special gifts, home decor, keepsakes and more!

Rustic Pillow Is Rooted in Fun

BURSTING with northwoods appeal, this cozy throw pillow (pictured at left) will liven up a window seat or rocking chair in no time. To make it, designer Loretta Mateik of Petaluma, California covered a purchased pillow form with Polarfleece trimmed with a flannel pine tree.

MATERIALS NEEDED:
Pattern at right
Tracing paper and pencil
7-inch x 9-inch piece of dark green flannel for tree applique
10-inch square of off-white Polarfleece
Two 15-inch squares of off-white-and-green plaid Polarfleece
All-purpose thread—dark green and off-white
Seven 1/2-inch two-hole buttons
White six-strand embroidery floss
Embroidery needle
One 1-inch gold metallic star-shaped button
Four 1-inch off-white two-hole buttons
14-inch square pillow form
Standard sewing supplies

FINISHED SIZE: Pillow measures about 14 inches square.

DIRECTIONS:
Hand-wash dark green flannel fabric. If water is discolored, wash again until rinse water runs clear. Dry and press fabric.

Trace tree pattern at right onto tracing paper as directed on pattern.

Pin pattern to dark green flannel fabric with grain lines matching. Cut out tree shape.

Center tree right side up on right side of 10-inch off-white Polarfleece square.

With dark green thread, zigzag around outside edge of tree shape.

Center the off-white Polarfleece square right side up on the right side of one 15-inch square of plaid Polarfleece. With off-white thread, zigzag around outside edge of the 10-inch off-white square.

Referring to photo at left for position and using off-white thread, hand-sew a 1-inch white button to each corner of appliqued top. In the same way, hand-sew star button to top of tree.

Separate six-strand floss and thread embroidery needle with four strands. Referring to photo at left for position, hold a 1/2-inch button on tree where desired. Insert needle from front to back through one hole in button, leaving a tail of thread on the front. Insert needle from back to front through opposite hole in button. Tie the thread ends together in a double overhand knot. Trim ends, leaving a 1/2-inch tail of floss. In the same way, randomly sew remaining 1/2-inch buttons to tree.

Pin appliqued front and remaining 15-inch plaid Polarfleece square together with right sides facing and edges matching. Sew around outside edge with a 1/2-inch seam, leaving an opening along one edge for turning. Clip corners diagonally.

Turn pillow right side out through opening. Insert pillow form. Turn raw edges of opening in. With matching thread, hand-sew opening closed. ❄

TREE PATTERN
Trace 1—tracing paper
Cut 1—dark green flannel

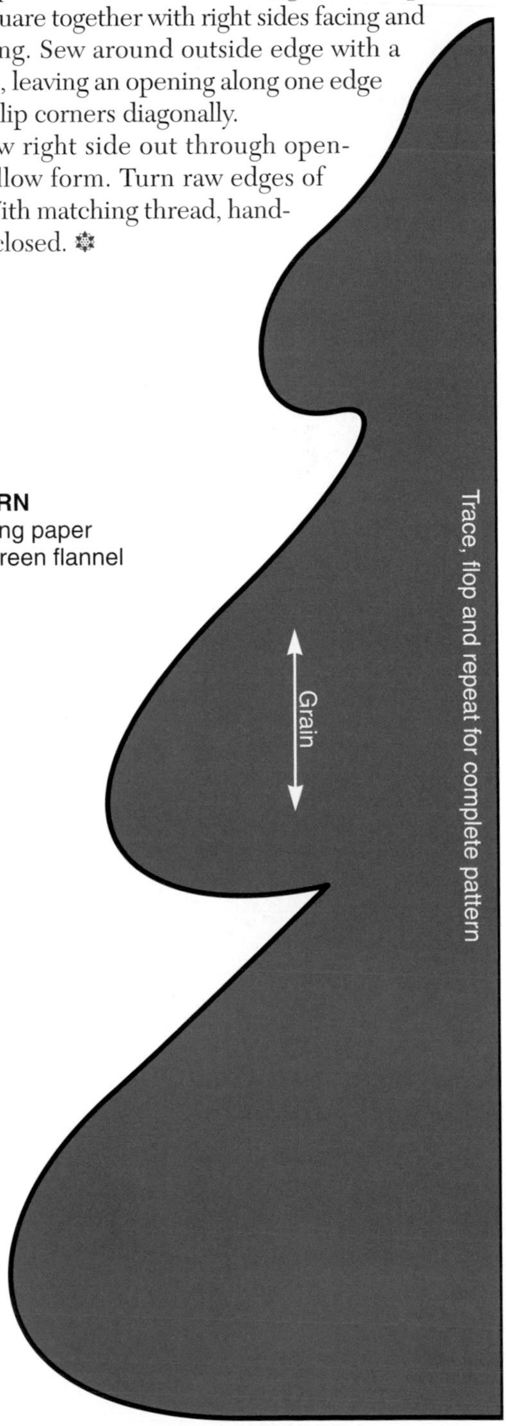

Grain
Trace, flop and repeat for complete pattern

Jolly Old Elf Stars On Simple Trim

INSPIRED by the notion of wishing upon a star, as well as the joy that Christmas brings, Penny Duff of Kennebunk, Maine created a cross-stitched ornament (pictured at left) that's fit for the season. The simple Santa holding a string of twinkling stars is a cinch to stitch.

MATERIALS NEEDED:

Chart below
Two 6-inch squares of off-white 14-count Aida cloth
DMC six-strand embroidery floss in colors listed on color key
Size 24 tapestry needle
Polyester stuffing
Scissors

FINISHED SIZE: Excluding hanging loop, ornament measures about 3 inches wide x 3-7/8 inches high. Cross-stitched design area is 38 stitches wide x 48 stitches high and measures about 2-5/8 inches wide x 3-3/8 inches high.

SANTA ORNAMENT CHART

COLOR KEY	DMC
⊡ White	
☐ Light Shell Pink	224
■ Medium Red	304
▣ Rose	335
▦ Dark Pistachio Green	367
▣ Light Pistachio Green	368
⊙ Pearl Gray	415
⊡ Light Old Gold	676
☐ Very Light Old Gold	677
▨ Medium Garnet	815
☒ Very Light Peach Flesh	948
◈ Gold Metallic (1 strand)	5282
BACKSTITCH	
— Black Brown (1 strand)	3371
FRENCH KNOT	
֍ Black Brown (2 strands)	3371
RUNNING STITCH	
— White	

Fig. 1

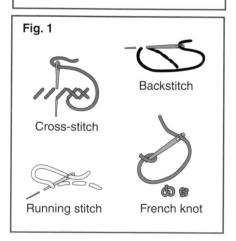

Cross-stitch

Backstitch

Running stitch

French knot

DIRECTIONS:

CROSS-STITCHING: Zigzag or overcast the edges of one piece of Aida cloth to prevent fraying. To find the center point, fold this piece in half lengthwise, then fold it in half crosswise and mark where the folds intersect.

Draw lines across the chart, connecting opposite arrows. Mark where lines intersect. Begin stitching here for a centered design.

Each square on the chart represents one set of fabric threads surrounded by four holes. Each stitch is worked over one set of threads with the needle passing through the holes.

The color and/or symbol inside each square on the chart, along with the color key, tells which color of six-strand embroidery floss to use to make cross-stitches and where to make gold metallic cross-stitches. Wide lines on the chart show where to work backstitches. Dashed lines show where to work running stitches. See color key for French knot symbol. See Fig. 1 for stitch illustrations.

Use 18-inch lengths of floss. Longer strands tend to tangle and fray. Separate the strands of floss and thread the needle with three strands for floss cross-stitches. Use two strands of floss for French knots and use one strand for all backstitches and gold metallic cross-stitches. Use unseparated floss for running stitches.

To begin stitching, leave a 1-inch tail of floss on back of work and hold tail in place while working the first few stitches over it. To end stitching, run the needle under a few stitches in back before clipping the floss close to work.

When all stitching is complete, and only if necessary, gently wash the stitched piece in lukewarm water. Press right side down on a terry towel to dry.

ASSEMBLY: Place stitched piece right side up on top of an unstitched piece of Aida cloth with edges even.

Thread needle with unseparated white floss. Stitch the two pieces together, stitching through every other square one square outside the entire cross-stitched area and stuffing the ornament as you stitch.

Trim the excess Aida cloth from the assembled ornament, cutting through both layers two squares out from the white stitching.

For hanging loop, thread needle with a 10-inch length of gold metallic floss. On the back of the ornament, stitch in and out of one square at each top corner. Remove needle and knot ends of metallic thread together. ❊

Painted Shovel Digs Into the Season

A FLURRY of smiles will pile up on your doorstep when you bring out this colorful mini shovel (pictured at right) during December. Alise Duerr, the designer of this decoration, hails from Merritt Island, Florida—which explains the sentiment behind the words on her shovel!

MATERIALS NEEDED:
Pattern on page 76
Tracing paper and pencil
Graphite paper
Stylus or dry ballpoint pen
6-inch-wide x 15-1/2 inch-high unfinished galvanized
  snow shovel
Paper towels
Water container
Foam plate or palette
Acrylic craft paints (Alise used Delta Ceramcoat
  paints)—Magnolia White, Midnight Blue and
  Nightfall Blue
Paintbrushes—large flat and No. 2 liner
Metal primer (Alise used Delta Metal Primer)
Satin varnish (Alise used Delta Satin Varnish)
Two 1/8-inch-thick x 3-inch-high wooden snowflake
  cutouts with drilled hole
15-inch length of silver cording to fit through drilled
  hole in wooden snowflakes
White dimensional fabric/craft paint
Fine glitter
Scissors

FINISHED SIZE: Shovel measures 6 inches wide x 15-1/2 inches high.

DIRECTIONS:
Keep paper towels and container of water handy to clean brushes. Place small amounts of paint as needed onto foam plate or palette. Add coats of paint as needed for complete coverage. Let paint dry after every application. Refer to

(continued on next page)

pattern below right and photo on page 75 as a guide while painting as directed in the instructions that follow.

Use flat brush and Midnight Blue to paint handle.

Use flat brush and metal primer to basecoat front of shovel.

Use flat brush and Nightfall Blue to paint front of shovel.

Use copy machine to enlarge pattern to 200% and trace pattern onto tracing paper, or mark tracing paper with a 1-inch grid and draw pattern as shown onto tracing paper.

Place traced pattern on front of shovel and slip graphite paper between pattern and shovel. Trace over lettering and snowflake pattern with stylus or dry ballpoint pen to transfer design onto shovel.

Use liner and Magnolia White to paint lettering, adding dots of paint to the letters where shown on pattern.

When lettering is dry, use flat brush to apply satin varnish to front of shovel and to handle following manufacturer's instructions. Let dry.

Use white dimensional fabric/craft paint to paint snowflake. While paint is still wet, sprinkle glitter over paint. Shake off excess glitter. Let dry.

Use flat brush and Magnolia White to paint all sides of each wooden snowflake. While paint is still wet, sprinkle snowflakes with glitter. Shake off excess glitter. Let dry.

Thread silver cording through drilled hole in each snowflake. Tie a knot close to each end of the cording. Trim excess cording close to knot. Slide a snowflake toward each end of cording. Tie cording in a bow around handle. ❄

Enlarge pattern 200%   Each square = 1 inch

"LET IT SNOW" SHOVEL PATTERN
Trace 1—tracing paper
Paint as directed in instructions

Frosty Place Card Brightens the Table

KNOW why this snowy dining accent (pictured above) is glowing with cheer? Crafter Nance Wilhite-Kueneman of Caldwell, Idaho used a burned-out lightbulb to make it!

MATERIALS NEEDED:
Standard lightbulb
Water container
Paper towels
Foam plate or palette
Acrylic craft paints (Nance used Delta Ceramcoat paints)—Black, Pink Frosting, Pumpkin and White
Iridescent glitter glaze (optional)
Paintbrushes—3/4-inch flat and small round
Black fine-line marker
15-inch length of black craft wire
Needle-nose pliers
Knit sock—red or desired color
24-inch length of heavy string
Glue gun and glue sticks
Scissors
Ruler
2-inch x 2-1/2-inch piece of white card stock
Medium black marker

FINISHED SIZE: Lightbulb snowman place marker measures about 2-1/2 inches wide x 6-3/4 inches high without the place card.

DIRECTIONS:
Keep paper towels and container of water handy to clean brushes. Place small amounts of paint as needed onto foam plate or palette. Add coats of paint as needed for complete coverage. Let paint dry after every application. Refer to photo above left as a guide while painting as directed in the instructions that follow.

Using flat brush and White, paint entire lightbulb.

If desired, apply glitter glaze to lightbulb following manufacturer's instructions. Let dry.

Use needle-nose pliers to carefully wrap one end of wire piece around socket end of lightbulb, securing the wire in place. Then shape the opposite end of wire in a flat spiral to hold place card.

From cuff end of sock, cut a 3-1/2-inch-wide circle-shaped band for snowman's hat and a 3/4-inch-wide circle-shaped band for scarf.

Glue 3/4-inch-wide band for scarf to bulb end of lightbulb so that lightbulb can stand upright.

Slip 3-1/2-inch-wide band over wire place card holder and socket end for hat. Wrap heavy string around hat about 3/4 inch from cut end and tie ends in a small bow. Spot-glue bow to hat. Glue bottom edge of hat to lightbulb as needed to hold, leaving about 1-1/2 inches of lightbulb showing for snowman's face.

Dip end of paintbrush handle into Black and dab on two small dots for eyes.

Using round brush and Pumpkin, paint a small circle for the nose.

Using round brush and Pink Frosting, paint two larger circles for cheeks.

Use black fine-line marker to add mouth.

Use medium black marker to write "For Santa" or a name on card stock piece. Slip card stock into spiraled wire. ✿

Angelic Pin Gets Right to the Point

WHETHER *it's a teacher, relative or really good friend, there's always someone who deserves extra recognition. This cheery cherub (pictured at right) is the perfect way to acknowledge all they do! "It's just right for that 'heaven-sent' someone," shares Tammy LeBlanc of Geismar, Louisiana.*

MATERIALS NEEDED:
1-1/4-inch-high x 1-1/4-inch-wide x 1/8-inch-thick
   purchased wooden square
Two 1/2-inch-high x 1/8-inch-thick purchased
   wooden hearts
5/8-inch-diameter domed-top wooden furniture plug
Water container
Paper towels
Foam plate or palette
Acrylic craft paints (Tammy used Apple Barrel paints)—
   Creamy Peach, Light Pink, Pure Gold Metallic, Satin
   Cream and White
Paintbrushes—small flat and liner
Toothpick
Cotton swab
Black fine-line permanent marker
Iridescent glitter
8-inch length of 1/4-inch-wide gold mesh ribbon
6-inch length of gold craft wire for halo
1-inch pin back
Glue gun and glue sticks
Scissors

FINISHED SIZE: Angel pin measures about 1-1/2 inches wide x 1-3/8 inches high.

DIRECTIONS:
Keep paper towels and container of water handy to clean brushes. Place small amounts of paint as needed onto foam plate or palette. Add coats of paint as needed for complete coverage. Let paint dry after every application. Refer to photo above right as a guide while painting and assembling as directed in the instructions that follow.

Use flat brush and Satin Cream to paint edges and one

side of wooden square.

Mix equal parts of Creamy Peach and White together to make a light flesh color. Use mixed paint and flat brush to paint sides and top of furniture plug for angel's head.

Use flat brush and White to paint edges and one side of each heart. While paint is still wet, sprinkle hearts with iridescent glitter. Shake off excess glitter. Let dry.

Use marker to write "Angel in disguise" in lower right part of painted square, adding dots to letters as shown in photo.

Use liner and Pure Gold Metallic to randomly add small stars to front of square.

Dip cotton swab into Light Pink and remove excess paint on paper towel. With a nearly dry swab and a circular motion, add cheeks to angel's head.

Use marker to add eyes, nose and mouth to angel's head.

Dip toothpick into White and add a tiny dot to each eye. In the same way, add a White dot to each cheek.

Glue angel's head on an angle to upper left corner of painted square.

Glue the two hearts below the angel's head so that the points of the hearts meet.

Tie gold mesh ribbon into a small bow. Trim ends as desired. Glue bow to points of hearts below angel's head.

Form gold wire into a small circle for halo. Glue halo to top of angel's head.

Glue pin back to back of square. Let dry. ✿

Nordic Ornaments Add a Dash of Drama

WITH RICH DETAIL and striking colors, these Scandinavian-inspired trims (pictured at left) will make quite a statement on your tree. Darlene Polachic of Saskatoon, Saskatchewan used counted cross-stitch to execute her idea.

MATERIALS NEEDED (for both):
Charts on this page and next page
Two 4-inch squares of white 14-count Aida cloth
DMC six-strand embroidery floss in colors listed on color key
Size 24 tapestry needle
Two 4-inch squares of lightweight white cotton fabric for back of ornaments
Polyester stuffing
1 yard of 1/8-inch white cord
Two 1-1/2-inch-long white tassels
White all-purpose thread
Standard sewing supplies

FINISHED SIZE: Each ornament measures about 4 inches wide x 6 inches high including hanging loop and tassel. Design area of each is 39 stitches x 39 stitches and measures about 2-3/4 inches square.

DIRECTIONS:
Zigzag or overcast edges of Aida cloth to prevent fraying.

Fold one square of Aida cloth in half lengthwise, then fold it in half crosswise and mark where the folds intersect.

To find the center of the chart, draw lines across the chart, connecting opposite arrows. Begin counting where the lines intersect to locate the first stitch of the top row, then locate the same spot on the Aida cloth and begin stitching there for a centered design.

Each square on the chart represents one set of fabric threads surrounded by four holes. Each stitch is worked over one set of threads with the needle passing through the holes.

The color and/or symbol inside each square, along with the color key, tells which color of embroidery floss to use to make the cross-stitches. See Fig. 1 below for stitch illustration.

Use 18-inch lengths of floss. Longer strands tend to tangle and fray. Separate the strands and thread the tapestry needle with three strands for all stitching.

To begin stitching, leave a 1-inch tail of floss on back of work and hold the tail in place while

NORDIC ORNAMENT CHART NO. 1

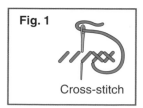

Fig. 1

Cross-stitch

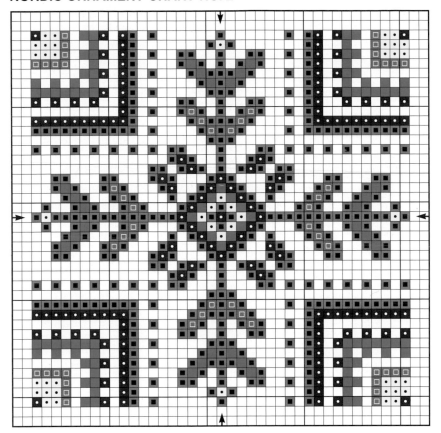

COLOR KEY	DMC
■ Black	310
■ Very Dark Pistachio Green	319
◨ Holiday Red	321
▣ Dark Wedgwood	517
⊡ Light Straw	3822

tly wash the stitched piece in lukewarm water. Press right side down on a terry towel to dry.

ASSEMBLY: Center each completed cross-stitched design wrong side up on a 4-inch square of white cotton backing fabric. Sew around each, stitching just outside the cross-stitched design and leaving an opening along one edge for turning.

Trim seams to 1/4-inch outside stitching. Trim corners diagonally. Turn each ornament right side out.

Stuff each ornament. Turn raw edges of openings in. With matching thread, hand-sew openings closed.

FINISHING: Cut length of cord in half. Thread hand-sewing needle with white thread. Starting at one corner, hand-sew a length of cord around outside edge of a stuffed ornament, making a small loop of cord at one corner for hanging loop. Join the raw edges of cord at the beginning corner. Hand-sew a white tassel to the corner opposite the hanging loop.

In same way, attach cord to remaining ornament. ❀

working the first few stitches over it. To end stitching, run the needle under a few stitches in back before clipping the floss close to work.

When all stitching is complete, and only if necessary, gen-

Santa Tree Trim Is on a Roll

TREAT your favorite cook to an ornament she'll appreciate by whipping up this rolling pin Santa (pictured at right) from Irene Wegener of Corning, New York. "You can easily make a bunch in just an evening or two," she says.

MATERIALS NEEDED:
7-inch-long wooden rolling pin
1/4-inch domed-top wooden furniture plug for nose
Paper towels
Water container
Foam plate or palette
Acrylic craft paints (Irene used Delta Ceramcoat)—
   Black, Black Cherry, Fleshtone, Rouge and White
Paintbrushes—1/2-inch flat and 1/4-inch flat
Ruler and pencil
Toothpick
Black fine-line permanent marker

(continued on next page)

Matte or satin varnish
White (tacky) glue
1/2-inch-wide x 5-inch-long piece of white felt or white
    100% cotton quilt batting
White loopy doll hair
Artificial pine sprig and red berry
Drill with 1/8-inch bit
8-inch length of green crochet thread or heavy thread
    for hanger
Scissors

FINISHED SIZE: Rolling pin Santa ornament measures about 1-1/2 inches wide x 7 inches high without hanger.

DIRECTIONS:
Keep paper towels and container of water handy to clean brushes. Place small amounts of paint as needed onto foam plate or palette. Add coats of paint as needed for complete coverage. Let paint dry after every application.

Refer to photo on page 79 as a guide while painting as directed in the instructions that follow.

Use 1/2-inch flat brush and Black Cherry to paint entire rolling pin.

Use ruler and pencil to draw a 1-1/2-inch wide x 1-3/4-inch long oval on one end of the rolling pin for Santa's face.

Use 1/4-inch flat brush and Fleshtone to paint the face and the 1/4-inch wooden furniture plug for nose.

Use 1/2-inch flat brush and White to paint a 1/2-inch-wide band around the top handle for the top of Santa's hat. Wipe excess paint off on paper towel so brush is nearly dry, then draw paintbrush down around the bottom edge of the band to make a blurred, uneven edge.

Glue flat side of painted nose to center of Santa's face. Let dry.

Dip end of a paintbrush handle into Black and add two small dots above nose for eyes.

Dip toothpick into White and add a tiny dot to each eye for highlight.

Dip 1/4-inch flat brush into Rouge and wipe excess paint off on paper towel. With a nearly dry brush and a circular motion, add cheeks and a bit of color to the tip of Santa's nose.

Apply matte or satin varnish following manufacturer's instructions. Let dry.

Use marker to add eyebrows above eyes.

For Santa's hair, wrap loopy doll hair around four fingers about eight times. Slip looped doll hair off fingers. Tie center of loops with another strand of doll hair to hold. Cut ends of loops. Glue center of bundle to top of painted oval, allowing strands to fall on each side of Santa's face.

For Santa's beard, wrap loopy doll hair around four fingers about 25 times. Slip looped doll hair off fingers. Tie center of loops with another strand of doll hair to hold. Cut ends of loops. Glue center of bundle to face just below nose, allowing strands to form beard.

Glue strip of white felt or white cotton quilt batting around top of rolling pin for trim of hat, covering center top of hair and overlapping ends of strip in back. Trim excess.

Glue artificial pine sprig and red berry to hat trim.

Trim Santa's hair and beard as desired.

Drill a hole from side to side through top handle of the rolling pin about 1/2 inch from the end of the handle. Insert one end of green crochet cotton or heavy thread through drilled hole. Knot ends together to form hanging loop. ❀

Snowman Pins Down the Season

LIKE FROSTING on a cake, this snowy accessory (pictured at left) will finish off an outfit or coat so sweetly. "I like to use different fabrics and felt for the hat and scarf so that each snowman is unique," says Bette Veinot of Bridgewater, Nova Scotia.

MATERIALS NEEDED:
Pattern on next page
Tracing paper and pencil
Two 3-inch x 5-inch pieces of white knit (sweatshirt)
    fabric
1-1/2-inch-high x 2-1/2-inch-wide piece of blue knit
    ribbing for stocking cap
All-purpose thread—blue and white
3/8-inch-wide x 6-inch-long piece of blue print
    Polarfleece for scarf
1-inch pin back
Polyester stuffing
Water container
Paper towels

Foam plate or palette
Acrylic craft paints—black, gold metallic, orange
  and red
Small flat paintbrush
Toothpick
Textured snow medium
Wooden craft stick
Iridescent glitter
Glue gun and glue sticks
Standard sewing supplies

FINISHED SIZE: Pin measures about 1-1/2 inches wide x 3 inches high.

DIRECTIONS:
SNOWMAN: Trace snowman pattern at right onto tracing paper with pencil.

Pin the white knit fabric pieces together with right sides facing and edges matching. With grain lines matching, pin snowman pattern to the white knit fabric. Sew around the outside edge of snowman pattern with a short straight stitch, leaving top open for turning where shown on pattern. Cut snowman out, cutting 1/8 inch outside stitching. Clip curves. Turn snowman right side out.

Stuff snowman firmly. Turn raw edges of opening in and hand-sew opening closed with matching thread.

PAINTING: Keep paper towels and container of water handy to clean brushes. Place small amounts of paint as needed onto foam plate or palette. Let paint dry after every application. Refer to pattern and photo on previous page as a guide while painting as directed in the instructions that follow.

Dip toothpick into black and dab two small dots onto snowman's head for the eyes. In the same way, add five tiny dots for the mouth.

Dip toothpick into orange and add a small triangle for nose.

Dip paintbrush into red and wipe excess paint onto paper towel. With a nearly dry brush and a circular motion, add snowman's cheeks.

Referring to photo for placement, paint a small gold metallic heart on the lower left-hand side of snowman as follows: Use toothpick to dab on two small dots of gold metallic paint as shown in Fig. 1 above right. While the paint is still wet, use toothpick to pull the paint down from each dot to form point of heart.

STOCKING CAP: Fold blue knit ribbing piece in half crosswise to make a 1-1/2-inch-high x 1-1/4-inch-wide piece. Sew long edges together with a narrow seam to make a tube. Turn tube right side out.

Roll up one raw edge of the blue knit tube twice to form brim of stocking cap.

Place stocking cap on snowman's head with seam in back and pull cap down around sides of snowman's head as shown in photo.

Hand-gather top of stocking cap together and tie a length of blue thread about 3/8 inch from top to hold.

Spot-glue stocking cap in place as needed to hold.

SCARF: Wrap the blue print Polarfleece for scarf around

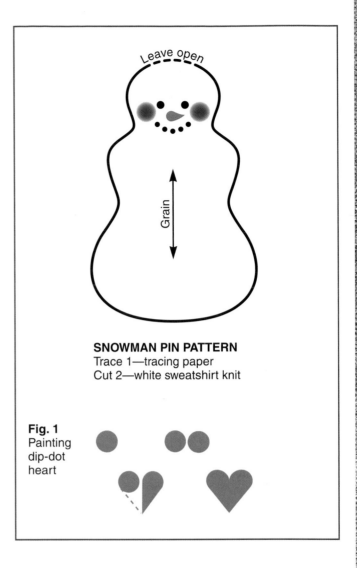

SNOWMAN PIN PATTERN
Trace 1—tracing paper
Cut 2—white sweatshirt knit

Fig. 1
Painting
dip-dot
heart

the snowman's neck and tie ends in an overhand knot.

Spot-glue ends of scarf to front of snowman.

FINISHING: Glue pin back centered vertically on back of snowman.

Use craft stick to apply textured snow to top and brim of hat. While still wet, sprinkle snow with iridescent glitter. Shake off excess glitter. Let dry.

Apply a bit of glue to ends of scarf and spread glue with craft stick. While glue is still wet, sprinkle glue with iridescent glitter. Shake off excess glitter. Let dry. ❁

Extra Idea

Want a snowman family to accent your home? Use a photocopier to enlarge the snowman pattern above to 200%, 300% and 400% to make a 6-, 9- and 12-inch-high snowman. Add plastic doll pellets to the bottom of each before stuffing them and adjust the size of the scarf and hat pieces proportionately. Then add twig arms and group the trio together to complete the scene.

Framed Wreath Has Festive Spirit

USING a pair of timeless holiday images—a brightly shining candle and a beribboned wreath—Country Woman Craft Editor Jane Craig stitched a wall hanging (pictured above) that will grace your home for many years to come.

MATERIALS NEEDED:
Patterns on next page
Tracing paper and pencil
Paper-backed fusible web
Compass
44-inch-wide 100% cotton fabrics—3/4 yard of unbleached muslin for circle background and backing, 1/2 yard of small green-on-off-white print for background square, 1/4 yard of green holly print for inner border and holly leaves, 1/4 yard of small off-white-on-green print for outer border and holly leaves, 1/8 yard of red print for inner border and candle trim, and scrap of red solid for candle
Scrap of yellow felt for candle flame
Black all-purpose thread and thread to match fabrics
Quilter's ruler
Quilter's marking pen or pencil
Rotary cutting tools (optional)
Lightweight cardboard
Rub-on glue stick
Glue gun and glue sticks
Red grosgrain ribbon—2-1/2 yards of 1-inch-wide ribbon for frame and 3 yards of 1/2-inch-wide ribbon for bow
Four 3/4-inch-deep x 1-5/8-inch-wide x 22-inch-long stretcher bars or 22-inch square frame

Stapler and staples
Standard sewing supplies

FINISHED SIZE: Framed wreath measures about 22 inches square.

DIRECTIONS:
CUTTING: Either use quilter's marking pen or pencil and ruler to mark fabrics before cutting them with a pencil or use rotary cutting tools to cut the fabrics. Cut fabric strips crosswise from selvage to selvage.

From unbleached muslin, cut one 26-inch square for backing and one 16-inch square for lining of circle background.

From green-on-off-white print, cut a 16-inch square for background square.

From green holly print, cut two 2-1/2-inch x 14-1/2-inch strips and two 2-1/2-inch x 18-1/2-inch strips for inner border.

From red print, cut four 1-1/2-inch x 18-1/2-inch strips for folded inner border.

From off-white-on-green print, cut two 4-inch x 18-1/2-inch strips and two 4-inch x 26-inch strips for outer border.

BACKGROUND: With edges matching, pin 16-inch square of green-on-off-white print fabric right side up to 16-inch square of muslin. Smooth out any wrinkles and sew around outside edges to hold pieces together.

Use compass to draw an 8-1/4-inch circle onto tracing paper. Cut out circle for pattern.

Center and pin the circle pattern to the right side of the 16-inch green-on-off-white print background square. Use quilter's marking pen or pencil to trace around the circle pattern. Remove pattern. Sew around traced circle with a small zigzag stitch. Cut a slit in the center of the green-on-off-white fabric circle only. Cutting close to the zigzag stitching, cut out the circle from the center of the green-on-off-white background fabric only, leaving a circle of muslin fabric showing.

With circle centered, trim background fabric to a 14-1/2-inch square.

CANDLE: Trace candle, candle trim and candle flame patterns on next page onto paper side of fusible web, leaving at least 1/2 inch between shapes. Cut shapes apart, leaving a margin of paper around each.

With grain lines matching, fuse shapes to wrong side of fabrics as directed on patterns. Cut out each shape following pattern lines.

Referring to photo above left for position, fuse candle to edge of background circle.

Fuse candle trim to top of candle with straight edges matching. Fuse flame 1/2 inch above top of candle.

Stitch between bottom of flame and top of candle with black thread and a narrow satin stitch for the wick.

With matching thread, satin-stitch around candle, candle trim and flame.

PIECING: Do all stitching with right sides of fabrics together, edges even, matching thread and an accurate 1/4-inch seam allowance. Press seams toward darker fabric unless instructions say otherwise.

FRAMED WREATH PATTERNS

HOLLY LEAF
Trace 1—tracing paper
Cut 1—lightweight cardboard
Cut 7—fused green holly print
Cut 7—fused off-white-on-green small print

CANDLE FLAME
Trace 1—paper-backed
　　　　fusible web
Cut 1—yellow felt

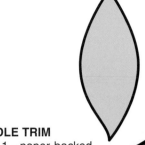

STEM

APPLIQUE KEY
—— Outline/cutting line
— Inside design line
←→ Direction of grain

Fig. 1
Adding holly leaves

Note: Patterns are given in reverse so they will face the correct direction when appliqued to the background.

CANDLE TRIM
Trace 1—paper-backed
　　　　fusible web
Cut 1—fused red
　　　　print

CANDLE TRIM

CANDLE
Trace 1—paper-backed fusible web
Cut 1—fused red solid

Inner border: Sew a 2-1/2-inch x 14-1/2-inch green holly print strip to opposite sides of background square. Open and press seams.

Sew a 2-1/2-inch x 18-1/2-inch green holly print strip to top and bottom of background square. Open and press seams.

Folded border: Fold each 1-1/2-inch x 18-1/2-inch red print strip in half lengthwise with wrong sides facing.

Pin a folded strip to opposite sides of the inner border with edges matching. Sew in place with a scant 1/4-inch seam. Do not press open.

In the same way, attach remaining folded strips to the top and bottom edges of the inner border.

Outer border: Sew a 4-inch x 18-1/2-inch off-white-on-green print strip to opposite sides of the folded border. Trim ends even with top. Open and press.

In the same way, sew the 4-inch x 26-inch strips to top and bottom edges of folded border. Open and press.

HOLLY LEAVES: Trace holly leaf pattern above onto tracing paper with pencil. Using rub-on glue stick, glue traced pattern to lightweight cardboard piece. Cut out holly leaf following pattern lines to make a template.

Fuse a 6-inch x 15-inch piece of paper-backed fusible web to a slightly larger piece of green holly print. Remove paper

(continued on next page)

backing and place fused side down on a same-size piece of green holly print to make a fused fabric sandwich.

In the same way, make a same-size fused fabric sandwich from off-white-on-green small print fabric.

Using quilter's marking pen or pencil, trace around holly template seven times on each fused fabric piece. Cut out each following pattern outline.

With matching thread, sew down the center vein of each holly leaf where shown on pattern.

Press the vein of each holly leaf with tip of iron, gently stretching each as you press to shape the holly leaves.

ASSEMBLY: Frame: Assemble stretcher frame to make a 22-inch square frame.

Place frame on a flat surface. Center 26-inch square of muslin for backing over frame. Starting at the center of each side, wrap fabric around to back and staple to back of frame to hold. Trim excess fabric from back of frame.

In the same way, staple pieced background centered right side up to frame.

Wreath: Referring to Fig. 1 on page 83, pin the holly leaves around the edge of the muslin circle, alternating the prints and tucking the stem end of each under the previous leaf to overlap them as needed to form a circle. When pleased with the arrangement, apply a thin bead of glue to the center vein of each and adhere the leaves to the background, leaving the outer edges and tips of each free. Let dry.

Bow: Cut 1/2-inch-wide red grosgrain ribbon into four 27-inch lengths. Working with all lengths as one, tie ribbon into a small bow.

With matching thread, hand-sew center of bow to bottom center of holly wreath.

Ribbon Frame: Place framed wreath right side up on a flat surface. Starting at center bottom of frame, glue 1-inch-wide grosgrain ribbon around outside edge of frame, keeping bottom edge of ribbon even with back of frame. Overlap ends and trim excess ribbon. ❁

Stay a Step Ahead With Frosty Friend

THIS CUTE CHARACTER (pictured above) will melt hearts during the holidays and keep your home brimming with cheer well into the New Year. Country Woman Craft Editor Jane Craig notes, "The entire project can be completed in a few hours."

MATERIALS NEEDED:
Patterns on next page
Tracing paper
Pencil
9-inch x 12-inch piece of black felt for hat
Men's white over-the-calf tube sock (Jane used Hanes brand)
3-inch Styrofoam ball for snowman's head
Firm roll of toilet tissue for snowman's body (Jane used Scott brand)
Clear plastic wrap to cover roll of toilet tissue
6-inch length of string or twist tie
Two black glass straight pins or small black beads for snowman's eyes
Three black buttons
1-1/4-inch-long piece of 1/4-inch wooden dowel for snowman's nose
Sandpaper
Small flat paintbrush
Orange acrylic paint
3/4-inch-wide x 20-inch-long torn strip of red print fabric for scarf
1/4-inch-wide x 7-1/2-inch-long strip of red fabric or ribbon for trim on hat
10-inch-length of 1/8-inch-wide green satin ribbon for bow on hat
Two 1/2-inch-long pinecones for trim on hat
Two small twigs for arms
Textured snow medium
Spray glitter or snow (optional)
Glue gun and glue sticks
Snowman accessories of your choice (Jane glued an artificial Christmas tree made from wired pine garland to her snowman)
Standard sewing supplies

FINISHED SIZE: Snowman measures about 7 inches wide x 9 inches high.

DIRECTIONS:

Trace hat top and hat brim patterns below onto tracing paper with pencil as directed on patterns.

Cut a hat top and hat brim piece from black felt. Also cut a 2-inch-wide x 7-1/4-inch-long piece from black felt for center band of hat.

Sew narrow ends of center band of hat together with a 1/4-inch seam to make a tube. Finger-press seam open.

With right sides facing, sew one edge of band piece to hat top piece.

With right sides facing, sew opposite edge of band piece to inside edge of hat brim piece. Turn hat right side out.

Sand one end of wooden dowel piece to make a cone shape for nose. Paint dowel piece orange for nose. Let dry.

Wrap roll of toilet tissue with clear plastic wrap. Slip wrapped tissue roll into top of sock. Insert Styrofoam ball into top of sock for head. Pull sock up to cover ball. Push foot end of sock into opening on opposite end of tissue roll. Adjust sock as needed so knit design of sock is straight and is the same over the roll of tissue and the snowman's head.

Tie top of sock together on top of head with string or twist tie. Glue as needed to hold. Trim excess sock if desired.

Glue felt hat to top of snowman's head.

Wrap narrow band of fabric or ribbon around hat near brim. Overlap ends in back and trim excess. Spot-glue as needed to hold trim in place.

Tie green ribbon into a small bow. Glue to hat where desired. Glue pinecones to center of bow.

Glue black beads on head or insert black glass straight pins into head and glue in place for eyes.

Cut a tiny hole in the front of head below eyes for nose. Apply glue to the flat end of the snowman's nose and insert nose into hole.

Glue buttons down front of snowman.

Wrap fabric for scarf around snowman's neck. Trim ends as desired. Spot-glue scarf to snowman as needed to hold.

Glue trims and accessories to snowman where desired.

Apply textured snow to hat, nose, buttons and accessories as desired. Let dry. Spray snowman with glitter or snow if desired. Let dry. ❀

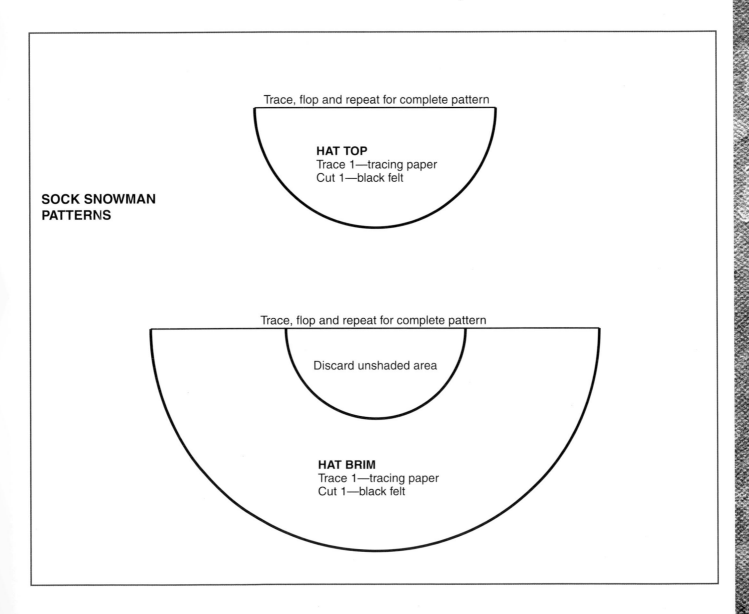

SOCK SNOWMAN PATTERNS

Trace, flop and repeat for complete pattern

HAT TOP
Trace 1—tracing paper
Cut 1—black felt

Trace, flop and repeat for complete pattern

Discard unshaded area

HAT BRIM
Trace 1—tracing paper
Cut 1—black felt

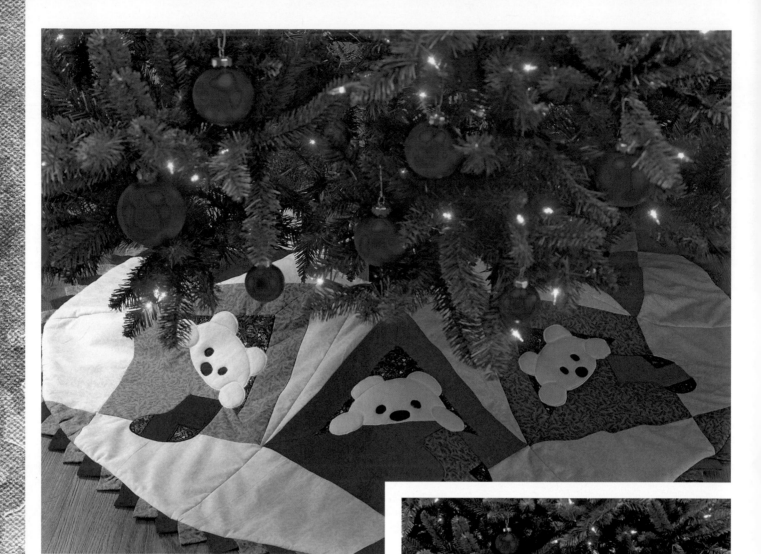

Holiday Tree Skirt Is 'Beary' Merry

THERE'S no skirting the issue—this quilted tree wrap (pictured above) is a creature comfort for the Christmas tree. Gretchen Eder of Delavan, Wisconsin stitched this reversible skirt that will brighten your pine from the bottom up.

MATERIALS NEEDED:
Patterns on pages 87 and 89
Tracing paper and pencil
Paper-backed fusible web
44-inch-wide 100% cotton fabrics—1-1/4 yards of small off-white print for pieced background and binding; 1 yard of small green print for blocks, stockings and prairie points; 1 yard of small red print for blocks, stockings and prairie points; 2 yards of dark coordinating print for backing, blocks and stockings and 1/8 yard or scrap of black solid for appliqued eyes and noses of bears
1/4 yard of 60-inch-wide off-white fleece for bear appliques

All-purpose thread to match fabrics
45-inch x 60-inch piece of lightweight quilt batting
Six 8-1/2-inch x 11-inch pieces of tear-away stabilizer or typing paper
Quilter's ruler
Quilter's marking pen or pencil
Rotary cutter and mat (optional)
Standard sewing supplies

FINISHED SIZE: Tree skirt measures about 42 inches across.

TREE SKIRT PATTERNS

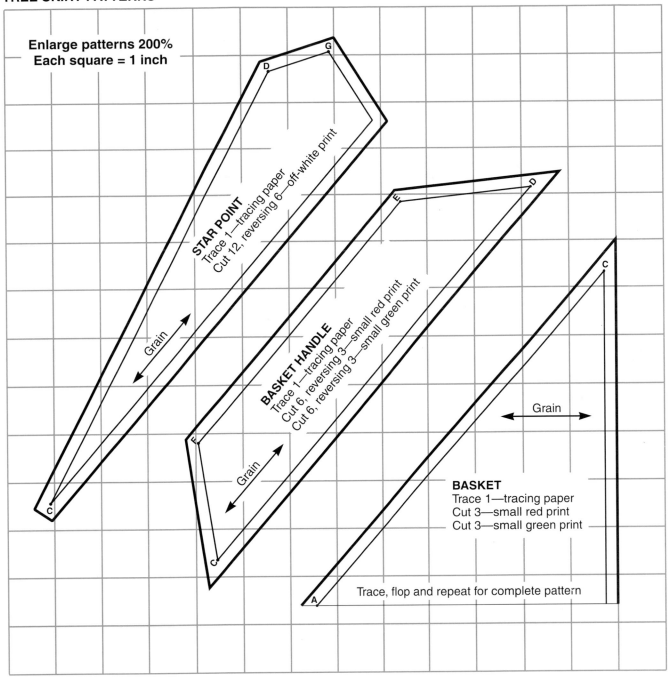

Enlarge patterns 200%
Each square = 1 inch

STAR POINT
Trace 1—tracing paper
Cut 12, reversing 6—off-white print

Grain

BASKET HANDLE
Trace 1—tracing paper
Cut 6, reversing 3—small red print
Cut 6, reversing 3—small green print

Grain

Grain

BASKET
Trace 1—tracing paper
Cut 3—small red print
Cut 3—small green print

Trace, flop and repeat for complete pattern

DIRECTIONS:

Wash the cotton fabrics without fabric softeners, washing each color separately. If the water from any fabric is discolored, wash again until the rinse water runs clear. Dry and press fabrics.

CUTTING: Either use quilter's marking pen and pencil to mark the fabrics before cutting them with a scissors or use rotary cutting tools to cut the pieces as directed in the instructions that follow.

Use copy machine to enlarge all patterns on pages 87 and 89 to 200%. Or mark tracing paper with a 1-inch grid and draw all patterns as directed onto tracing paper, making sure to transfer all letters and dots.

Cut out fabric pieces as directed on patterns, matching grain lines and marking dots carefully.

For prairie point edging, cut out fifty 3-inch squares each of small red print fabric and small green print fabric.

Cut a 2-1/4-inch-wide x 44-inch-long strip of off-white print for binding and ties.

PIECING: Do all piecing with right sides of fabrics together, edges even and dots matched as directed. Use matching thread and accurate 1/4-inch seams. Press seams toward darker fabric unless directions say otherwise.

Basket base unit (make 6): Pin an off-white bottom corner piece to one A-B edge of a red or green print basket base

(continued on next page)

piece, matching dots A and B. Stitch from the A dot to the B edge. In the same way, sew a reversed bottom corner piece to opposite A-B edge of same red or green print basket base piece.

Sew the A-C edges of a matching red or green print basket piece to the A-C edges of off-white bottom corner piece, stitching from the A dot to the C edge on each.

Repeat to make a total of three red print and three green print basket base units.

Basket handle unit (make 6): Pin an off-white star point piece to the long edge of a red or green print basket handle piece, matching dots C and D. Stitch from C edge to D edge. In the same way, sew a reversed off-white star point piece to a matching reversed print basket handle piece. Then sew the joined pieces together, stitching from the G edge to the E dot.

With dots E and F matching, sew the E-F edges of an inside basket piece to the E-F edges of red or green print basket handle, stitching from the E dot to the F edge on each side.

Repeat to make a total of three red print and three green print basket handle units.

Tree skirt section (make six): Pin a matching basket base unit and basket handle unit together, matching dots C and C at opposite ends. Stitch from C edge to C edge.

Pin each tree skirt section right side up to batting. Cut out each, roughly following outside edge of each tree skirt section.

Stitch around each piece, stitching 1/4 inch from outside edge of sections.

Cut along outside edges to trim away excess batting.

APPLIQUE: Trace bear, stocking, heel and toe patterns onto paper side of fusible web as directed on patterns, leaving at least a 1/2 inch space between shapes. Cut shapes apart, leaving a margin of paper around each.

Following manufacturer's instructions and with grain lines matching, fuse shapes onto wrong side of fabrics as directed on patterns. Transfer inside design lines on each bear by straight-stitching along pattern lines. Cut out shapes following outlines of patterns. Remove paper backing.

Referring to patterns and photo on page 86 for position, pin a bear to each tree skirt section, placing paws and face of bear just below the seam between the basket base unit and the basket handle unit piece. Slip the upper right-hand corner of a contrasting stocking under the bear's paw. Fuse stocking in place.

Keeping bear in position, turn entire tree section over and fuse bear in place from wrong side.

Turn tree skirt section over and fuse heel and toe pieces and nose and eye pieces in place, being careful not to flatten the fleece fabric.

Place stabilizer or typing paper behind applique. Using matching thread, satin-stitch around edges of fused pieces and over inside design lines. Remove stabilizer or paper. Pull all loose threads to the back and secure.

Repeat to make six appliqued tree skirt sections.

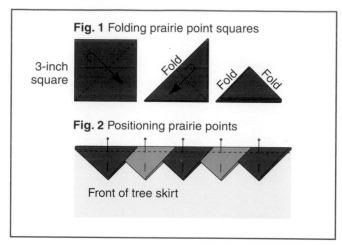

Fig. 1 Folding prairie point squares
3-inch square   Fold   Fold   Fold

Fig. 2 Positioning prairie points
Front of tree skirt

ASSEMBLY: Place appliqued tree skirt sections right side up on a flat surface, alternating red and green print baskets to form a circle.

Sew long edges of sections together, leaving one seam unstitched for opening. Trim as needed to make a smooth circle on outside and inside edges.

PRAIRIE POINT EDGING: Referring to Fig. 1 above, fold a 3-inch red or green print square in half with wrong sides facing to make a triangle. Fold the triangle in half to make a smaller triangle with raw edges even. Press triangle and pin to hold. Repeat with all remaining red and green print squares, making a total of 100 folded triangles for prairie points.

Pin a green prairie point to the right side of the outside edge of tree skirt with double-folded edge about 1/2 inch from the straight edge of the opening. Referring to Fig. 2 above, pin a red prairie point, inserting it as shown. In the same way, add remaining prairie points, alternating the colors as shown. Baste pieces in place, stitching a scant 1/4 inch from raw edges.

BACKING: Place remaining backing fabric right side up on a flat surface. Place tree skirt wrong side up on top of backing, aligning open edges with grain of fabric. Smooth out layers. Pin as needed to hold.

Cut away the excess backing, following the outer edges of tree skirt.

Stitch around outer edges of tree skirt with a 3/8-inch seam, starting at the top of one open edge and ending at the top of the other open edge, leaving center circle unstitched.

Turn tree skirt right side out though open center circle. Press as needed.

BINDING AND TIES: Fold and press binding strip in half lengthwise with wrong sides together.

Center binding strip on wrong side of tree skirt center circle with raw edges even and ends extending evenly. Stitch binding strip to center circle with a 1/4-inch seam. Fold in cut edges and ends 1/4 inch and press. Fold binding strip in half again, encasing raw edges of center circle and forming ties. Stitch close to final folded edges to hold binding in place and to form ties. ❄

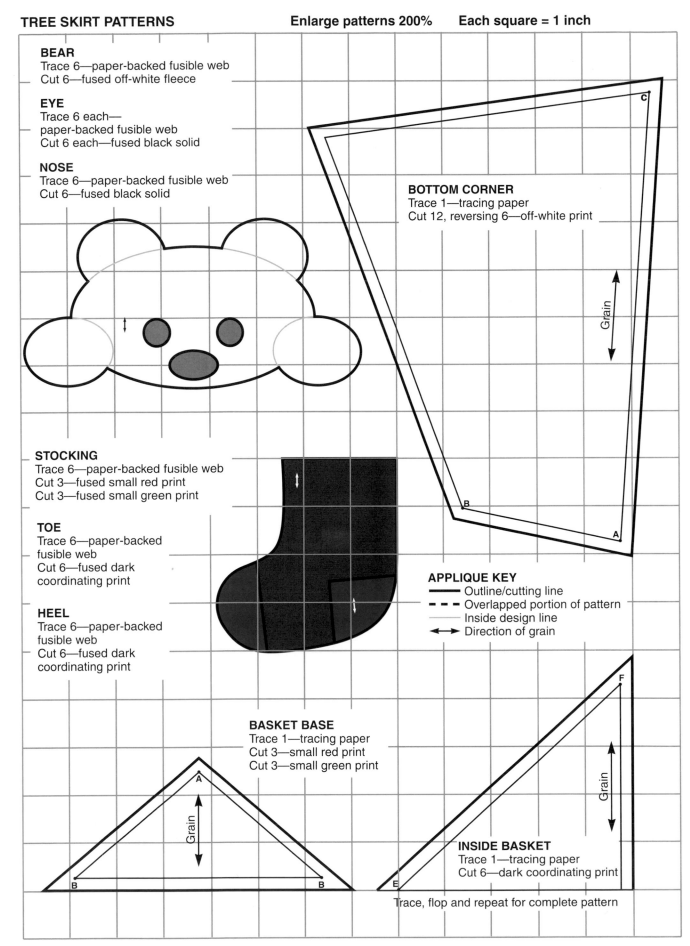

TREE SKIRT PATTERNS

Enlarge patterns 200%   Each square = 1 inch

BEAR
Trace 6—paper-backed fusible web
Cut 6—fused off-white fleece

EYE
Trace 6 each—
paper-backed fusible web
Cut 6 each—fused black solid

NOSE
Trace 6—paper-backed fusible web
Cut 6—fused black solid

BOTTOM CORNER
Trace 1—tracing paper
Cut 12, reversing 6—off-white print

Grain

STOCKING
Trace 6—paper-backed fusible web
Cut 3—fused small red print
Cut 3—fused small green print

TOE
Trace 6—paper-backed
fusible web
Cut 6—fused dark
coordinating print

HEEL
Trace 6—paper-backed
fusible web
Cut 6—fused dark
coordinating print

APPLIQUE KEY
—— Outline/cutting line
– – – Overlapped portion of pattern
—— Inside design line
◄—► Direction of grain

BASKET BASE
Trace 1—tracing paper
Cut 3—small red print
Cut 3—small green print

Grain

INSIDE BASKET
Trace 1—tracing paper
Cut 6—dark coordinating print

Grain

Trace, flop and repeat for complete pattern

Perky Penguin Dives Into the Holidays

STRAIGHT from the South Pole comes this cute crocheted bird (pictured above). Beverly Mewhorter of Apache Junction, Arizona suggests replacing the bead eyes with felt or crocheted bobbles if you'll be giving this critter to an infant or toddler.

MATERIALS NEEDED:
Worsted-weight yarn—1.5 ounces of black and small
   amounts each of red, white and yellow
Size H/8 (5mm) crochet hook
Polyester stuffing
Two 1/4-inch black beads or black buttons for the
   penguin's eyes
Yarn or tapestry needle
Scissors

FINISHED SIZE: Penguin measures about 6 inches wide x 10 inches high.

DIRECTIONS:
BODY: B-Round 1: With black, ch 4 for first dc, work 11 dcs in first ch made, join with a sl st in third ch of beginning ch-4: 12 dcs.

B-Round 2: Ch 3 for first dc, dc in same st, work 2 dcs in each remaining st around, join with a sl st in top of beginning ch-3: 24 dcs.

B-Round 3: Ch 3 for first dc, dc in same st, dc in next st, [work 2 dcs in next st, dc in next st] around, join with a sl st in top of beginning ch-3: 36 dcs.

B-Rounds 4-8: Ch 3 for first dc, dc in each st around, join with a sl st in top of beginning ch-3: 36 dcs.

B-Round 9: Ch 3 for first dc, dc next 2 sts tog, [dc in next st, dc next 2 sts tog] around, join with a sl st in top of be-

ginning ch-3: 24 sts.

B-Round 10: Ch 2, [dc next 2 sts tog] around, join with a sl st in top of first dc: 12 sts. Stuff body.

B-Round 11: Ch 2, dc in next dc, [dc next 2 sts tog] around, join with a sl st in top of first dc: 6 sts. Fasten off.

HEAD: H-Round 1: With black, ch 4 for first dc, work 11 dcs in first ch made, join with a sl st in third ch of beginning ch-4: 12 dcs.

H-Round 2: Ch 3 for first dc, dc in same st, work 2 dcs in each remaining st around, join with a sl st in top of beginning ch-3: 24 dcs.

H-Rounds 3-5: Ch 3 for first dc, dc in each st around, join with a sl st in top of beginning ch-3: 24 dcs.

H-Round 6: Ch 2, dc in next st, [dc next 2 sts tog] around, join with a sl st in top of first dc: 12 sts. Stuff head.

H-Round 7: Ch 2, dc in next dc, [dc next 2 sts tog] around, join with a sl st in top of first dc: 6 sts. Fasten off.

Using black yarn and yarn or tapestry needle, join head and body by sewing last round of head centered over last round of body.

WINGS (make two): With black, ch 13, dc in fourth ch from hk for first two dcs, dc in each ch across to last ch, work 6 dcs in last ch, dc in 9 chs on opposite side of beginning ch: 25 dcs. Fasten off.

Referring to photo above left for placement, use yarn or tapestry needle and black yarn to sew straight edge of a wing to opposite sides of top of body.

BELLY PIECE: BP-Round 1: With white, ch 4 for first dc, work 11 dcs in first ch made, join with a sl st in third ch of beginning ch-4: 12 dcs.

BP-Round 2: Ch 3 (counts as first dc here and throughout), dc in same st, work 2 dcs in each remaining st around, join with a sl st in top of beginning ch-3: 24 dcs.

BP-Round 3: Ch 3, dc in same st, dc in next st, [work 2 dcs in next st, dc in next st] around, join with a sl st in top of beginning ch-3: 36 dcs. Fasten off.

Referring to photo for placement, use yarn or tapestry needle and white yarn to sew belly piece centered on front of body.

FACE PIECE: FP-Round 1: With white, ch 4 for first dc, work 11 dcs in first ch made, join with a sl st in third ch of beginning ch-4: 12 dcs.

FP-Round 2: Ch 3 for first dc, dc in same st, work 2 dcs in each remaining st around, join with a sl st in top of beginning ch-3: 24 dcs. Fasten off.

Referring to photo for placement, use yarn or tapestry needle and white yarn to sew face piece centered on front of the head.

BEAK: With yellow, ch 4, dc in fourth ch from hk, (dc, ch 2, sl st) in same ch. Fasten off.

Referring to photo for placement, use yarn or tapestry needle and yellow yarn to sew beak to center of face piece.

FEET (make two): F-Row 1: With yellow, ch 4, work 4 dcs in fourth ch from hk, turn.

F-Row 2: Ch 3, dc in same st, dc in each of next 3 sts, work 2 dcs in last st. Fasten off.

Referring to photo for placement, use yarn or tapestry needle and yellow yarn to sew feet to Round 3 of body.

HAT: Round 1: With red, ch 35, join with a sl st in first ch made to form a ring, ch 3 (counts as first dc here and throughout), dc in each st around, join with a sl st in top of beginning ch-3: 35 dcs.

Round 2: Ch 3, dc in each st around, join with a sl st in top of beginning ch-3: 35 dcs.

Round 3: Ch 3, dc in next st, [dc next 2 sts tog, dc in next st] around, join with a sl st in the top of beginning ch-3: 24 sts.

Round 4: Ch 3, [dc next 2 sts tog, dc in next st] around, join with a sl st in top of beginning ch-3: 16 sts.

Round 5: Ch 3, [dc in next st, dc next 2 sts tog] around, join with a sl st in top of beginning ch-3: 11 sts.

Round 6: Ch 3, dc in each st around, join with a sl st in top of beginning ch-3: 11 dcs.

Round 7: Ch 1, [sc next 2 sts tog] around to last st, sc in last st, join with a sl st in beginning ch-1: 6 sts.

Round 8: [Ch 14, sl st in first ch] three times, * sl st in next st, [ch 14, sl st in same st] three times; repeat from * around: 15 ch-14 loops. Fasten off, leaving a tail of yarn. Thread yarn through sts of Round 8 and pull yarn to close opening. Fasten off.

SCARF: With red, ch 75, dc in fourth ch from hk and in each remaining ch across, ch 2, sl st in last ch. Fasten off.

FINISHING: Place hat on penguin's head. Use yarn or tapestry needle and red yarn to sew hat in place.

Use yarn or tapestry needle and black yarn to sew beads or buttons to head above beak for eyes.

Tie scarf around penguin's neck.

Use yarn or tapestry needle to weave in loose ends. ❁

CROCHET ABBREVIATIONS

ch(s)	chain(s)
hk	hook
dc(s)	double crochet(s)
sc(s)	single crochet(s)
sl st	slip stitch
st(s)	stitch(es)
tog	together

* [ ] Instructions following asterisk or between brackets are repeated as directed.

( ) Instructions between parentheses are all worked in stitch or space indicated.

Country Cherub Is Heaven Sent

THIS GRACEFUL GAL (pictured above) gives a spiritual touch to any setting. What's more, adds Charlotte Rickard of Spartanburg, South Carolina, the angel is stuffed with whole spices, making her an aromatic addition to your decor.

MATERIALS NEEDED:
Patterns on page 92
Tracing paper and pencil
Tea bag and 1 cup of boiling water
Tan all-purpose thread
Polyester stuffing
Black acrylic craft paint
Toothpick
Glue gun and glue sticks
White (tacky) glue
Standard sewing supplies
Two 6-inch x 16-inch pieces of tea-dyed muslin (see note)
1 cup of whole spices (Charlotte used cloves, allspice and cinnamon chips)
8-inch x 18-inch piece of blue-and-tan check fabric
3-ply jute string—twelve 5-inch lengths and six 9-inch lengths
2-inch grapevine wreath for halo
6-inch grapevine bow for wings

NOTE: To tea-dye muslin, steep a tea bag in boiling water. Remove tea bag. Place muslin in tea and remove when desired color is reached. Dry and press tea-dyed muslin.

FINISHED SIZE: Angel measures about 6 inches wide x 10 inches high.

DIRECTIONS:
Use copy machine to enlarge patterns to 200%, or mark tracing paper with a 1-inch grid and draw patterns as shown onto tracing paper.

HEAD/BODY: Place the two 6-inch x 16-inch pieces of tea-dyed muslin together with edges matching. Pin angel head/body and base pattern pieces to fabric. Cut out pieces

(continued on next page)

as directed on patterns, cutting along the outline of the patterns.

With a 1/4-inch seam, sew around curved edges of head/body piece, leaving opening on one side only where shown on pattern. Pin base piece to bottom of body piece, matching notches to side seams. Sew base piece to bottom of head/body piece with a 1/4-inch seam. Clip curves. Turn head/body piece right side out through opening.

Pour spices into bottom of head/body piece. Stuff head/body piece firmly, making sure body stands upright. Turn raw edges of opening in. Whipstitch opening closed. See Fig. 1 at right for stitch illustration.

Dip toothpick into black paint. Dab two small dots for eyes on one side of angel's head. Let dry.

DRESS: Fold 8-inch x 18-inch piece of blue-and-tan check fabric in half crosswise. Sew narrow edges together with a 1/4-inch seam, making a large tube. Press seam open.

Sew around one long edge of tube with a gathering stitch about 1/2 inch from the edge.

Slip fabric tube over angel, placing gathered edge at angel's neck and seam in back. Draw up thread ends to gather fabric snugly around angel's neck. Fasten off. Use glue gun to spot-glue gathered edge to neck.

HAIR: Untwist the 5-inch-long pieces of jute string to separate the three plies. Apply white (tacky) glue to the top of the angel's head. Glue the pieces to the angel's head from front to back for bangs. Let dry.

Untwist the 9-inch-long pieces of jute string. Glue the pieces across the top of the angel's head and down each side of the angel's face as before. Let dry.

FINISHING: Using the glue gun, glue the 2-inch grapevine wreath to the top of the angel's head for the halo.

In the same way, glue the 6-inch grapevine bow to the back of the angel for the wings. ❀

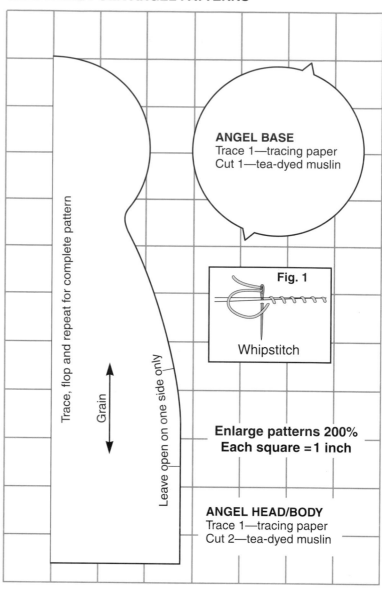

GRAPEVINE FOLK ANGEL PATTERNS

ANGEL BASE
Trace 1—tracing paper
Cut 1—tea-dyed muslin

Trace, flop and repeat for complete pattern

Grain

Leave open on one side only

Fig. 1

Whipstitch

**Enlarge patterns 200%
Each square = 1 inch**

ANGEL HEAD/BODY
Trace 1—tracing paper
Cut 2—tea-dyed muslin

Mini Boxes Are Big On Frosty Fun

TALK ABOUT thinking outside the box! Lenora Schut of Pella, Iowa came up with these fun papier-mache containers (pictured at left) for Christmas gift giving. "I like to put matching handmade snowman pins inside the boxes," she says.

MATERIALS NEEDED (for both):
Papier-mache boxes—one 2-inch square box and one
   1-1/2-inch x 2-1/2-inch rectangular box
1-3/8-inch-high split wooden snowman
1/8-inch-thick x 1-15/16-inch-high wooden snowman
   cutout
Water container
Paper towels

Foam plate or palette
Acrylic craft paints (Lenora used DecoArt Americana
paints)—Antique Gold, Burnt Umber, Lamp Black,
Leaf Green, Light French Blue, Neutral Grey, Primary
Red, Pumpkin, Sable Brown, Titanium White and
Williamsburg Blue
Paintbrushes—3/4-inch flat, small round and liner
Toothpick
Cotton swab
Black fine-line permanent marker
Newspaper to cover work surface
Toothbrush or spatter brush
Two 3/8-inch-wide x 4-inch-long strips of
green-red-and-white check fabric
Scissors
White (tacky) glue
Matte spray sealer

FINISHED SIZE: Square box measures 2 inches square x
1-3/8 inches high. Rectangular box measures 1-1/2 inches
wide x 2-1/2 inches long x 1-1/4 inches high.

DIRECTIONS:
Keep paper towels and container of water handy to clean
brushes. Place small amounts of paint as needed onto foam
plate or palette. Add coats of paint as needed for complete
coverage. Let paint dry after every application. Refer to photo on page 92 as a guide while painting as directed in the
instructions that follow.

SQUARE BOX: Bottom: Using round brush and
Williamsburg Blue, paint a narrow horizontal strip just above
the bottom edge of the box bottom.

Using flat brush and Williamsburg Blue, paint a vertical
stripe on each side of box bottom.

Using round brush, add narrow Titanium White and Antique Gold stripes to box bottom, creating a plaid design.

Top: Using flat brush, paint entire outside of box lid
Williamsburg Blue.

Using round brush, paint two tree trunks Sable Brown.

Using round brush and Leaf Green, add boughs to each
tree trunk.

Using round brush and Burnt Umber, add shading to
right side of each tree trunk and to bottom edges of each
bough.

Using flat brush and Titanium White, add a band of
snow along the edge below trees on top of lid using an up-
and-down motion. With a nearly dry brush, add a bit of Titanium White to the tree boughs.

Using flat brush, paint split snowman Titanium White.

Using flat brush, paint snowman's hat Neutral Grey.

Using round brush, add a narrow Antique Gold band
to hat.

Dip handle of paintbrush into Lamp Black and add two
small dots for snowman's eyes and three larger dots down the
front of the snowman for buttons.

Using liner, add a tiny Pumpkin triangle for snowman's
nose.

Using liner and Primary Red, paint a tiny heart on right-

hand side of snowman.

Dip toothpick into Titanium White and add a tiny dot to
each eye for highlights.

Use black marker to add snowman's mouth.

Dip cotton swab into Primary Red and wipe excess off
on paper towel. With a nearly dry cotton swab and a circular motion, add cheeks to snowman.

Place snowman, box lid and box bottom on newspaper-
covered surface.

Thin Titanium White with clean water to an ink-like
consistency. Dip toothbrush or spatter brush into thinned
paint. Hold brush about 6 inches above painted pieces and
draw your thumb or a paintbrush handle across bristles to
spatter-paint the pieces.

Apply matte spray sealer to box following manufacturer's
instructions.

Wrap a strip of fabric around snowman's neck for scarf.
Glue ends in place as needed to hold.

Glue snowman to top of box lid.

RECTANGULAR BOX: Using flat brush, paint entire
outside of box lid and box bottom Light French Blue.

Top: Using the round brush, paint two tree trunks Sable
Brown.

Using round brush and Leaf Green, add boughs to each
tree trunk.

Using round brush and Burnt Umber, add shading to
right side of each tree trunk and to bottom edges of each
bough.

Using flat brush and Titanium White, add a band of
snow along the edge below trees on top of lid using an up-
and-down motion. With a nearly dry brush, add a bit of Titanium White to the tree boughs.

Using flat brush, paint snowman cutout Titanium White.

Dip toothpick into Lamp Black and add two small dots for
snowman's eyes and nine larger dots down the front of the
snowman for buttons.

Using liner and Pumpkin, add a tiny triangle for snowman's nose.

Using liner and Primary Red, paint a tiny heart on right-
hand side of snowman.

Use black marker to add snowman's mouth and to shade
lower edge of nose.

Dip cotton swab into Primary Red and wipe excess off
on paper towel. With a nearly dry cotton swab and a circular motion, add cheeks to snowman.

Place snowman, box lid and box bottom on newspaper-
covered surface.

Thin Titanium White with clean water to an ink-like
consistency. Dip toothbrush or spatter brush into thinned
paint. Hold brush about 6 inches above painted pieces and
draw your thumb or a paintbrush handle across bristles to
spatter-paint the pieces.

Apply matte spray sealer to box following manufacturer's
instructions.

Wrap a strip of fabric around snowman's neck for scarf
and tie ends in an overhand knot.

Glue snowman to top of box lid. ❄

Knit Set Makes a Heartwarming Gift

WITH STITCHING that resembles traditional Aran knitting, this cozy hat and scarf (pictured above) from experienced knitter Nita Lucas of Reno, Nevada will delight almost anyone.

MATERIALS NEEDED (for both):
Off-white worsted-weight yarn—approximately 6 ounces for scarf and 3 ounces for hat
Knitting needles—size 10 (6mm) for scarf and size 8 (5mm) for hat (or sizes needed to obtain correct gauge)
Tape measure
Size H/8 (5mm) crochet hook
Scissors
3-inch square of cardboard
Yarn or tapestry needle

GAUGE: Working in St st (k on RS, p on WS) on size 10 needles, 15 sts and 20 rows = 4 inches. Working in St st (k on RS, p on WS) on size 8 needles, 15 sts and 22 rows = 4 inches.

FINISHED SIZE: Scarf is about 9-3/4 inches wide x 60 inches long without fringe. Hat has a 21-inch circumference.

DIRECTIONS:
SCARF: Cast on 37 sts.
Row 1 (RS): [K 1, yo, sl 1, k 1, psso, yo, k 1, sl 1, k 1, psso, k 1, k2tog, k 1, yo, k2tog, yo] twice, k 1, yo, sl 1, k 1, psso, yo, k 1, sl 1, k 1, psso, k 1, k2tog, k 1, yo, k2tog, yo, k 1: 37 sts.
Row 2 (WS): P across row: 37 sts.
Row 3: [K 2, yo, sl 1, k 1, psso, yo, sl 1, k 1, psso, k 1, k2tog, yo, k2tog, yo, k 1] twice, k 2, yo, sl 1, k 1, psso, yo, sl 1, k 1,

psso, k 1, k2tog, yo, k2tog, yo, k 2: 37 sts.
Row 4: P across row: 37 sts.
Repeat Rows 1-4 until piece measures 60 inches or desired length, ending with an odd numbered row.
Bind off in k 1, p 1 pattern across row. Fasten off.
Use crochet hook to weave in all loose ends.
Fringe: Cut 72 14-inch lengths of yarn. Fold one strand of yarn in half. Insert crochet hook into first stitch on one narrow edge of scarf. Draw fold of yarn through stitch on WS of scarf to make a loop and pull ends to tighten loop around yarn. Repeat to add 36 pieces of yarn fringe evenly spaced along both narrow ends of scarf. Trim ends even.

HAT: Cast on 96 sts.
Row 1: K 1, p 1 across: 96 sts.
Rows 2-8: K the k sts and p the p sts across, inc 1 st at end of Row 8: 97 sts.
Row 9 (RS): K 1, * yo, sl 1, k 1, psso, yo, k 1, sl 1, k 1, psso, k 1, k2tog, k 1, yo, k2tog, yo; repeat from * across, ending last repeat with k 1: 97 sts.
Row 10 (WS): P across row: 97 sts.
Row 11: K 2, * yo, sl 1, k 1, psso, yo, sl 1, k 1, psso, k 1, k2tog, yo, k2tog, yo, k 1; repeat from * across, ending last repeat with k 2: 97 sts.
Row 12: P across row: 97 sts.
Rows 13-40: Repeat Rows 9-12 seven times, dec 1 st at end of Row 40: 96 sts.
Row 41: * K2tog, p 1; repeat from * across: 64 sts.
Row 42: K 1, p 1 across: 64 sts.
Rows 43-44: Repeat Row 42: 64 sts.
Row 45: K2tog across: 32 sts.
Row 46: P across row: 32 sts.
Row 47: K2tog across: 16 sts.
Row 48: P across row: 16 sts.
Row 49: K2tog across: 8 sts.
Row 50: P across row: 8 sts.
Fasten off, leaving a 6-inch tail of yarn. Thread tail onto yarn or tapestry needle and insert through remaining sts. Pull yarn tight to draw up sts. Fold hat with RS together and ends matching. Use yarn to sew back seam.
Pom-pom: Wind matching yarn around 3-inch square of cardboard 50 times. Cut yarn at opposite edges of cardboard to make yarn pieces 3 inches long. Carefully remove cardboard. Tie another piece of yarn tightly around center of yarn pieces. Holding ends of tie, shake the pom-pom to fluff.
Thread ends of tie onto yarn or tapestry needle and sew pom-pom to top of hat. Fasten off. Trim ends as needed. ❁

KNIT ABBREVIATIONS			
dec	decrease	RS	right side
inc	increase	sl	slip
k	knit	st(s)	stitch(es)
p	purl	tog	together
psso	pass slipped	WS	wrong side
	stitch over	yo	yarn over

* [ ] Instructions following asterisk or between brackets are repeated as directed.

Sweet Trims Will Spice Up Your Tree

UNLIKE their cookie counterparts, these gingerbread men (pictured above) are sure to last all season long! Irene Wegener rolled out the fabric fellows for her Corning, New York home and shares the instructions so you can do the same.

MATERIALS NEEDED (for both):
Pattern on page 96
Tracing paper and pencil
Four 6-inch x 7-inch pieces of light brown solid fabric
Matching all-purpose thread
White pearl cotton or heavy thread
Embroidery needle
Polyester stuffing
3/16-inch-thick wooden cutouts—one 1-inch-high
   primitive star, one 1-1/2-inch-high gingerbread boy,
   one 1-inch-wide x 1-1/4-inch-high rectangle and one
   7/8-inch-high country heart
Water container
Paper towels
Foam plate or palette
Acrylic craft paints—black, dark brown, gold, light
   brown, off-white and red
Paintbrushes—small flat and liner
Toothpick
6-inch length of 19-gauge black craft wire
Needle-nose pliers
Drill with 1/8-inch bit
Satin varnish
Black fine-line permanent marker
Two 1-1/4-inch-wide x 12-inch-long torn strips of red
   small print fabric for scarves
9-inch length of wired pine garland
12-inch length of mini lights garland
Two 3/4-inch white gumdrop stars or buttons
Glue gun and glue sticks
Standard sewing supplies

FINISHED SIZE: Each gingerbread man measures about 6 inches wide x 6 inches high.

DIRECTIONS:
Trace pattern on page 96 onto tracing paper with pencil as directed on pattern. Cut out pattern on traced lines.

Pin two pieces of light brown fabric together with right sides facing and edges matching. Make a second set.

Pin complete gingerbread pattern to one fabric set with grain lines matching. With matching thread, sew around gingerbread with a short straight stitch. Repeat on remaining fabric set, making a second gingerbread.

Cut out each, cutting 1/4 inch outside stitching. Clip curves. Cut a small horizontal slit in one layer of fabric at the neck of each where shown on pattern. Turn each right side out through opening.

Stuff each gingerbread man firmly with polyester stuffing. Whipstitch edges of each opening together. See Fig. 1 on page 96 for stitch illustration.

Thread embroidery needle with white pearl cotton or heavy thread. Use pearl cotton or heavy thread and long straight stitches to add frosting to ends of arms and legs and to add hair to the top of each gingerbread man's head. See Fig. 1 for stitch illustration.

PAINTING: Keep paper towels and container of water handy to clean brushes. Place small amounts of paint as needed onto foam plate or palette. Add coats of paint as needed for complete coverage. Paint all sides of wooden pieces unless instructions say otherwise. Let paint dry after every application. Refer to photo above left as a guide while painting as directed in the instructions that follow.

Use flat brush and off-white to paint rectangle.

Use flat brush and gold to paint star.

Use flat brush and red to paint heart.

Use flat brush and light brown to paint wooden gingerbread boy.

Dip flat brush into light brown and wipe excess paint off on paper towel. With a nearly dry brush and light brown, drybrush one side of rectangle to give it an aged look.

Add a bit of clean water to light brown to thin it to an ink-like consistency. Use flat brush and thinned paint to shade the outside edges of the rectangle.

Dip flat brush into dark brown. Wipe excess paint off on paper towel. With an up-and-down motion, add a bit of dark brown to front of the wooden gingerbread boy and shade around the outside edges of the shape.

Use liner and off-white to add wavy frosting lines to the front of the wooden gingerbread boy.

Use liner and black to write "HOPE" on one side of the gold star and to write "SUGAR AND SPICE" on one side of the off-white rectangle.

Dip end of liner handle into black and add small dots to the ends of the letters.

Dip end of liner handle into black and add two tiny dots for eyes and three small dots for buttons to the wooden gingerbread boy. In the same way, add two small dots to each stuffed gingerbread man for eyes.

Use liner and black to add dashed lines around the edge

(continued on next page)

of the star, hearts and sign and to add eyebrows and mouth to wooden gingerbread boy.

Dip toothpick into off-white and add a tiny dot to the stuffed gingerbread men's eyes.

Dip flat brush into red and wipe excess paint off on a paper towel. With a nearly dry brush and a circular motion, add cheeks to gingerbread men and boys.

Use black marker to add eyebrows and a mouth to each stuffed gingerbread man.

Apply varnish to all wooden shapes following manufacturer's instructions. Let dry.

FINISHING: Wrap scarf strip around neck of each gingerbread man. Tie ends in an overhand knot. Trim ends as desired. Glue a gumdrop star or button to knot of each scarf.

Wrap mini lights garland around wired pine garland. Glue wrapped pine garland to front of a gingerbread man.

Drill a hole through the upper right-hand corner of the wooden rectangle. Insert wire piece through hole and use pliers to coil end of wire on front of rectangle. Insert opposite end of wire from back to front through the right hand of the gingerbread man without garland. Use pliers to coil end of wire as before to hold.

Referring to photo for position, glue hearts, star and wooden gingerbread boy to stuffed gingerbread men.

Using embroidery needle, attach a length of pearl cotton or heavy thread to top back of one gingerbread man's head. Knot ends together to form hanging loop. Cut ends close to knot. Repeat on remaining gingerbread man. ❋

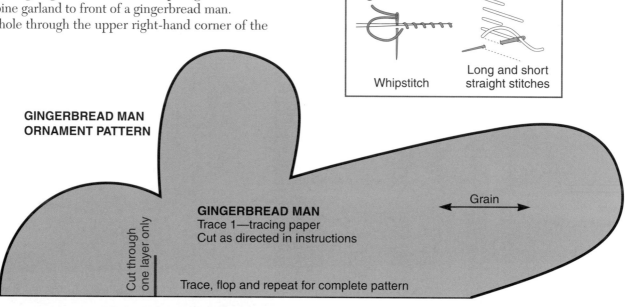

Fig. 1

Whipstitch

Long and short straight stitches

GINGERBREAD MAN ORNAMENT PATTERN

Cut through one layer only

GINGERBREAD MAN
Trace 1—tracing paper
Cut as directed in instructions

Grain

Trace, flop and repeat for complete pattern

Adorable Accent Bears Glad Tidings

HEADS are sure to turn when you deck your halls with this whimsical Christmas wreath (pictured at left). Liz Case of Hart, Michigan stitched a fun-for-all-ages teddy bear, then used that cute cub to decorate a gilded grapevine wreath.

MATERIALS NEEDED:
Patterns on next page
Tracing paper and pencil
Felt—two 9-inch x 12-inch pieces of dark brown and scrap of black (Liz used Kunin Rainbow Felt)
4-inch square of off-white cotton quilt batting
Dark brown all-purpose thread
Polyester stuffing
Black six-strand embroidery floss
Embroidery needle
Two 9mm animal eyes
12-inch gold metallic grapevine wreath
12-inch length of artificial wired pine garland

Eight dried and fully opened pinecones
18-inch length of 2-inch-wide coordinating
  wire-edge ribbon
1-inch-high x 1/8-inch-thick laser-cut wooden holiday
  greeting
Red acrylic craft paint
Small flat paintbrush
Six plastic liberty bells in desired colors
Craft wire
Glue gun and glue sticks
Scissors
Standard sewing supplies

FINISHED SIZE: Teddy bear wreath measures about 15 inches wide.

DIRECTIONS:
BEAR: Trace patterns below onto tracing paper as directed on patterns.

Cut shapes from felt and batting as directed on patterns.

Pin matching ear pieces together with right sides facing and edges matching. Sew around curved edge of each set with a narrow seam, leaving straight edge open. Clip curves. Turn each right side out.

Pin two matching head pieces together with right sides facing and edges matching. Sew around with matching thread and a 1/4-inch seam, leaving an opening for turning. Clip curves. Turn right side out.

Attach two animal eyes to front of head about 1-1/2 inches apart and about 1-1/2 inches from seam. Stuff head firmly. Turn raw edge of opening in and hand-sew opening closed.

With matching thread, hand-sew the straight edge of ears to the top of bear's head where shown on pattern.

Pin muzzle piece on the front of the bear's head. Thread embroidery needle with black six-strand embroidery floss. Stitch muzzle to bear's head with short straight stitches, stuffing muzzle as you stitch around. See Fig. 1 below for stitch illustration.

With black floss, make a long straight stitch down the center of bear's muzzle. Pull thread to make a slight indentation and fasten off. See Fig. 1 for stitch illustration.

Glue black felt nose piece to the top of bear's muzzle.

FINISHING: Use flat brush and red to paint wooden holiday greeting. Add coats of paint as needed for complete coverage, letting paint dry after every application.

When paint is dry, glue wooden holiday greeting to the top front of wreath.

Form ribbon into a small bow. Trim ends as desired. Glue bow below the muzzle of bear's head.

Wire artificial pine garland to bottom front of wreath. Glue bear head to center of garland. Glue four pinecones to each side of pine garland.

Glue bells to front of wreath in groups of three.

Attach a loop of wire to top back of wreath for hanger. ❄

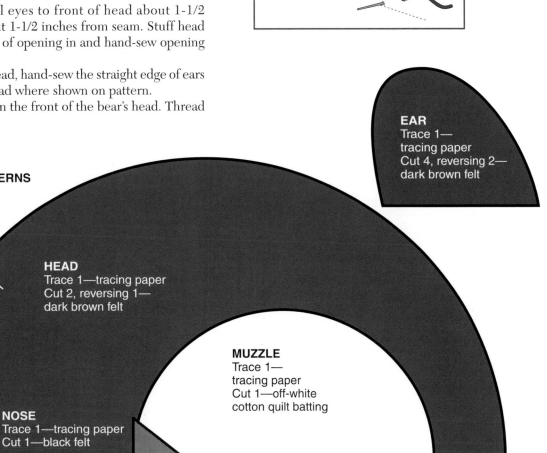

Fig. 1

Long and short straight stitches

EAR
Trace 1—
tracing paper
Cut 4, reversing 2—
dark brown felt

TEDDY BEAR WREATH PATTERNS

Placement of ear

HEAD
Trace 1—tracing paper
Cut 2, reversing 1—
dark brown felt

MUZZLE
Trace 1—
tracing paper
Cut 1—off-white
cotton quilt batting

NOSE
Trace 1—tracing paper
Cut 1—black felt

Trace, flop and repeat for complete patterns

The Joys of Jewelry

You'll love creating these beaded beauties for a sister, friend...or yourself!

Festive Fir Pins On Fashion Fun

COLORFUL BEADS and a zigzag of gold wire is just about all it takes to create this lovely evergreen accessory (pictured above at top left) from crafter Diane Hesse of Mt. Enterprise, Texas. Would you rather have a thinner tree? Or one with a bit more color? Simply adjust the number and position of the bends in the wire to change the shape of the tree and string additional colored beads onto the wire.

MATERIALS NEEDED:
15-inch length of 20-gauge gold craft wire
Twenty-one 3mm gold beads
14 assorted-color E beads (Diane used two light blue, two clear, three green, two orange, three red and two yellow E beads)
15mm red star bead
Tie-tack with clutch back
E-6000 or jewelry glue
Needle-nose pliers
Ruler
Wire cutters

FINISHED SIZE: Tree pin measures about 2-1/8 inches wide x 2-5/8 inches high.

DIRECTIONS:
Use needle-nose pliers to make a small loop at one end of the gold craft wire just big enough to fit around the wire on the back of the tie tack.

Hold the wire with the loop at the top. Referring to the photo above, use needle-nose pliers to bend the wire slightly to the right, then to the left about 1/4 inch from the loop. Add one gold bead, one E bead and one more gold bead to the wire. Slide the beads over to the last bend.

Bend the wire to the right about 1/2 inch from the first bend. Add a gold bead, one E bead and another gold bead to the wire. Slide beads over to the last bend.

Bend the wire to the left about 3/4 inch from last bend. Add two gold beads and one E bead as before. Slide beads over to last bend.

Bend the wire to the right about 1 inch from last bend. Add three gold beads and two E beads, alternating them as before. Slide the beads over to the last bend.

Bend the wire to the left about 1-1/4 inches from last bend. Add four gold beads and three E beads as before.

Bend the wire to the right about 1-1/2 inches from last bend. Add four gold beads and three E beads as before.

Bend the wire to the left about 1-3/4 inches from last bend. Add four gold beads and three E beads as before.

Slide the beads over to the last bend. Bend the wire to the right about 2 inches from last bend, then to the left about

1-1/2 inches from previous bend. Bend the wire back and forth at 1/2 inch lengths for tree trunk. Trim any excess wire.

Remove clutch back from post of tie tack. Insert the post end of the tie tack from front to back through the top loop of wire and glue to hold. Glue star bead to flat side of tie tack. Let dry.

Insert post of tie tack through clothing and replace clutch back to hold pin in place. ✿

Gem of a Bracelet Is Letter-Perfect

THIS SPARKLING ACCENT (pictured in center of photo at left) lets you wear your heart on your sleeve, thanks to the letter-block beads. You can arrange them any way you like to literally spell out your feelings! Kelly Van Sickle of Laurens, Iowa and her sister, Elaine, created the bracelet using beads in the birthstone colors of their siblings and chose the word "Sisters"...but you could also spell out "Mom" or "Love."

MATERIALS NEEDED:
Sterling silver beads—four 3mm round beads, eight
    4mm daisy spacer beads, two 3mm rondelle beads, six
    4mm rondelle beads and 4mm letter-block beads
    spelling "SISTERS"
Two 2mm sterling silver crimp tubes
Sixteen 3mm clear spacer beads
6mm bicone Swarovski crystal beads—two of each
    birthstone color representing each sister (see note)
One sterling silver toggle clasp
12-inch length of beading wire
Crimping tool or flat-nose pliers
Flush cutters or very sharp craft scissors
Needle-nose pliers (optional)
Bead design board (optional)

NOTE: Kelly used green, red, turquoise and two sets of light blue beads to represent five sisters. Clear bicone crystal beads could be substituted for the colored beads anywhere in the design if there are fewer sisters in your family.

FINISHED SIZE: Bracelet measures about 7 inches long.

DIRECTIONS:
On beading board or flat surface, lay out the letter-block beads to spell "SISTERS."

Place a 3mm rondelle bead at the beginning and end of the letter-block beads. Place a 4mm rondelle bead between each of the letter-block beads.

Place a 6mm bicone birthstone bead of each color on each side of the letter beads, placing the birthstone beads in order of birth from oldest to youngest. Place a clear spacer bead, a daisy spacer bead and a clear spacer bead between the birthstone beads.

At each end, add a 3mm round bead, a crimp tube and another 3mm round bead.

Thread one half of toggle clasp onto beading wire. Starting at one end, thread a round bead and crimp tube onto both ends of the beading wire, leaving a short piece of beading wire extended. Pull to fit bead snugly next to toggle clasp. Crimp the crimp tube closed with crimping tool or flat-nose pliers. Cut excess short end of beading wire.

Thread remaining beads onto wire in planned order.

Attach other half of toggle clasp to opposite end, threading beading wire through all beads. Crimp tube as before. Pull beading wire to fit beads together snugly. Crimp the crimp tube closed with crimping tool or flat-nose pliers. Cut excess short end of beading wire. ✿

Silver Necklace Has Holiday Luster

WANT to bedazzle a fashion-conscious friend this Christmas? Or need a graceful way to accessorize a dress? Try this elegant necklace (pictured at bottom in photo at left) from Jill Hackman of Snow Shoe, Pennsylvania. The technique is so easy, even a novice beader can create this piece in little time.

MATERIALS NEEDED:
Sterling silver beads—sixteen 2mm beads, sixteen 3mm
    beads, seven 5mm Bali beads and 160 (1mm x 4mm)
    liquid silver beads
Two 2mm sterling silver crimp beads
One sterling silver spring ring clasp with split ring
36-inch length of clear beading wire (Jill used Accuflex
    beading wire)
Flush cutters or very sharp craft scissors
Crimping tool or flat-nose pliers
Needle-nose pliers (optional)

FINISHED SIZE: Necklace measures about 17 inches long.

DIRECTIONS:
Thread clasp onto 36-inch length of beading wire and fold wire in half, creating two strands of equal length.

Thread both ends of wire through one crimp bead and push bead toward clasp until it is 1/8 inch from clasp. Crimp bead closed with crimping tool or flat-nose pliers.

Over both ends of wire, thread on one 3mm bead and one 2mm bead.

* Separate the two wires and thread 10 liquid silver beads on each wire. Bring both ends of wires together and thread on one 2mm bead, one 3mm bead, one Bali bead, one 3mm bead and one 2mm bead. Repeat from * six more times.

Separate the two wires. On each wire, thread 10 liquid silver beads. Bring wires together and thread on one 2mm bead, one 3mm bead and a crimp bead.

Thread both wires through the split ring and thread them back through the crimp bead (use needle-nose pliers if desired). Tuck the ends of wire into the 3mm bead. Clip off excess wire as close as possible to 3mm bead. Crimp the crimp bead closed using crimping tool or flat-nose pliers. ✿

Jingle Bell Earrings Ring in Christmas

YOU'LL spread cheer everywhere you go when you wear these jingling earrings (pictured at left in the photo on page 101) from Country Woman Craft Editor Jane Craig. They take mere moments to assemble but add lots of fun to the holidays. Want a matching necklace? Just choose a chain of any length, then string three matching bells onto the center.

MATERIALS NEEDED:
Two 10mm silver or gold jingle bells
Two silver or gold fish hook earrings (with bead and spring)
Needle-nose pliers

FINISHED SIZE: Each earring is about 1 inch long.

DIRECTIONS:
Use needle-nose pliers to open the loop on the bottom of each silver or gold earring. Slip a matching jingle bell on each loop. Use needle-nose pliers to close each loop.

To make a matching necklace, thread three jingle bells onto a necklace chain. (Use needle-nose pliers to remove and replace jump ring on end of chain if needed.) ❋

Necklace/Bracelet Is a Double Delight

YOU GET TWO gorgeous pieces of jewelry in one when you create this versatile accessory (pictured at bottom and inset in the photo on page 101). From Country Woman Craft Editor Jane Craig, it's a beaded strand that can be coiled into a chunky bracelet or looped around your neck as a single-strand necklace. Either way you wear it, the magnetic beads will hold it in place!

MATERIALS NEEDED:
Seventy 4mm silver tube beads
Eighteen 5mm x 8mm cut tube magnetic hematite beads
Sixty-eight 6/0 colored Czech glass E beads (Jane used Green Iris E beads)
Seventy 6/0 crystal silver-lined Czech glass E beads
Two silver crimp beads
Two silver head pins
36-inch length of beading wire (Jane used Beadalon 49-Bright .018 wire)
Wire cutters
Needle-nose pliers
Crimping pliers (optional)
Measuring tape

FINISHED SIZE: Beaded strand is about 31 inches long.

DIRECTIONS:
END BEAD (make two): String one crystal E bead and one silver tube bead on one head pin. Use needle-nose pliers to form a loop close to silver tube bead. Cut excess wire and use pliers to flatten and close the coiled head pin.

BEADING: Thread a crimp bead and the loop of one end bead onto one end of the beading wire. Bring the wire back through the crimp bead. Pull the beading wire tight, leaving a 34-inch-long tail of wire. Use crimping pliers or needle-nose pliers to secure crimp bead close to loop of end bead. Cut the short end of the wire close to crimp bead.

Thread beads on beading wire in the following order: one magnetic bead, one silver tube bead, one crystal E bead, one colored E bead, one crystal E bead, one silver tube bead, two colored E beads, one silver tube bead, one crystal E bead, one colored E bead, one crystal E bead and one silver tube bead. Add remaining beads in the same order, ending last repeat with a magnetic bead.

Thread remaining crimp bead on beading wire followed by the loop of the remaining end bead. Thread wire end through the crimp bead. Pull the end of beading wire, making sure all the beads touch along the wire. Use crimping pliers or needle-nose pliers to secure crimp bead close to loop of end bead. Cut the short end of the wire close to crimp bead. ❋

Poinsettia Pin Has Blooming Beauty

AS VIBRANT as the flower that inspired it, this sparkling poinsettia pin (pictured at top left in the photo below right) is the perfect accent for the holiday season. Diane Walters of Natrona Heights, Pennsylvania used glass seed beads and an unusual beading technique to make this striking accessory. Attach a pin back like she did…or turn the brooch into a flowery hairpin by gluing it to a barrette.

MATERIALS NEEDED:
Glass seed beads—one package (approximately 457) red beads, six yellow beads and three green beads
26-gauge gold wire
Hand-sewing needle
Wire cutters
Needle-nose pliers
Ruler
Green floral tape
1-inch pin back

FINISHED SIZE: Pin measures about 2-1/2 inches across.

DIRECTIONS:
Refer to photo at right as a guide while assembling the poinsettia as directed in the instructions that follow.

LARGE PETAL (make five): Measure and cut one 8-inch length and three 5-inch lengths of gold wire.

Wrap the end of a 5-inch length of wire tightly around hand-sewing needle two or three times to form a tiny circle of wire very close to one end of the wire. Slide wire off needle. Use wire cutters to cut any excess wire close to first loop. Use needle-nose pliers to flatten loop and make it smooth. Repeat with remaining two 5-inch lengths of gold wire, making three short wires with a loop at one end of each.

Fold the 8-inch length of wire in half and crimp the fold with the needle-nose pliers.

Add seven red seed beads to one end of the 8-inch length of wire. Insert the beaded end of the wire through the circle end of one 5-inch length of wire and then add 11 more red seed beads to the same end of the 8-inch piece. Add 10 red seed beads to the 5-inch length of wire.

Holding all beads in place, insert the opposite end of the 8-inch length of wire through the circle end of another 5-inch length of wire and position it at the fold of the 8-inch wire.

Hold the petal upside down and twist the ends of only the beaded wires together to hold the beads in place and to form the first half of a large petal.

On the other half of the 8-inch length of wire, add eight red seed beads, the last 5-inch length of wire and 10 more red seed beads. Add 9 red seed beads to the last 5-inch length of wire. Hold the petal upside down and twist the ends of only the beaded wires together.

Add 12 to 16 red seed beads to the center 5-inch length of wire for the center vein of the petal. Twist all the wires together, shaping the petal as desired.

Repeat to make a total of five large petals.

SMALL PETALS (make three): Cut a 6-inch length of gold wire.

Use needle-nose pliers to make a small loop at one end of the wire piece.

String 34 beads on the wire piece. Hold all the beads against the small loop and bend the wire between the ninth and tenth beads. The first nine beads will form the center of the petal. Shape the remaining beads around the center to form a petal. Wrap the wire end between the ninth and tenth beads to hold.

Repeat to make a total of three small petals.

CENTER (make three): Cut a 3-inch length of gold wire.

String one yellow, one green and another yellow seed bead onto wire. Hold the beads at the center of the length of wire. Twist the ends of wire together to hold the beads in place for beaded stem.

Repeat to make a total of three beaded stems.

Twist ends of all three beaded stems together for center of poinsettia.

ASSEMBLY: Twist the wire stems of the three small petals around the beaded center.

Twist the wire stems of the five large petals around the wire stems of the small petals.

Use wire cutters to cut wire stems about 1/2 inch from base of poinsettia.

Wrap wire end with floral tape and add pin back while wrapping the wires. Bend wire stem to the side so pin will lay flat when worn. ❈

Cheyenne looked so pretty in her BRIGHT red outfit. She was full of HOPE and anticipation for the holidays. When CHRISTMAS day finally arrived, we had so much to CELEBRATE.

Seasonal Scrapbooking

Preserve holiday memories with one designer's picture-perfect pages.

ESPECIALLY *for Christmastime, scrapbook enthusiast Mary Ayres of Boyce, Virginia assembled two merry pages for memory albums—a joyful journal design (pictured above) and a whimsical gift creation (pictured on page 103). You can easily make these pages for your own treasured Christmas photos... simply follow the step-by-step instructions here!*

Journal Page Tells A Christmas Story

MATERIALS NEEDED:

12-inch x 12-inch sheet of card stock for back of page
12-inch x 12-inch sheets of printed paper—textured gold, green floral, green dot and red check papers
Card stock scraps—light green, burgundy and dark green
Two gold hinges
One gold clasp
19 small gold paper fasteners
8 green eyelets
3/8-inch-wide gold metallic ribbon
4-inch x 6-inch photo

Sandpaper
Scrapbook glue
Gold ink pad
Scissors
Computer and printer for labels and journal entry
Ruler
1/16-inch and 3/16-inch circle punches

NOTE: Mary used Wild Asparagus Happy Holidays papers and Beacon Adhesives Zip-Dry glue.

FINISHED SIZE: Page is 12 inches square.

DIRECTIONS:

For the background of the page, glue a 5-inch x 12-inch piece of green dot paper to the right-hand edge of the card stock backing. Then glue a torn-edge 7-1/4-inch x 12-inch piece of dark green card stock to the left-hand edge and add a slightly smaller piece of green floral paper to same edge.

From burgundy card stock, cut a piece that is slightly larger than your photo. Frame that piece with a larger piece of red check paper. Sand the edges of the red check paper. Glue the frames and photo together to the floral paper.

Cut four large star shapes from the gold textured paper. Sand the edges of each star. Glue them down the right-hand side of the page.

Using a computer and printer, print "BRIGHT," "HOPE," "CHRISTMAS," "CELEBRATE" and your journal entry on light green paper. Cut the words out, leaving a small border around each. Sand and add antique ink to the edges of each. Glue a larger piece of green solid to the back of the journal piece to frame it.

Use paper fasteners to attach the word labels, hinges and clasp to the page. Fasten the eyelets to the page. Lace metallic ribbon through the eyelets and tie the ends in a bow. ❊

Gift Page Presents Photos Festively

MATERIALS NEEDED:
12-inch x 12-inch piece of card stock for back of page
Card stock—light blue, light yellow, light green, medium green, turquoise and white
Four different coordinating print papers for gifts
Four coordinating paper fasteners
Four photos
Scrapbook glue
Blue ink pad
Scissors
Computer and printer for labels and title section
Ruler

Sewing machine
Blue all-purpose thread
3/4-inch and 1/8-inch circle punches

NOTE: Mary used K&Company Kimberly Hodges papers and Zip-Dry Paper Glue from Beacon Adhesives.

FINISHED SIZE: Page is 12 inches square.

DIRECTIONS:
Cut a 6-inch square from light blue, light yellow, light green and medium green card stock. Glue squares side-by-side with edges meeting onto the 12-inch-square card stock piece for back of page. Sew a zigzag stitch along inside edges of squares. Glue thread ends to the back of page.

Use a computer to print the page title on turquoise card stock. Cut out the title and add blue ink to the edges for an antique look. Glue at an angle to the center of the page.

Cut a box shape from each of the four different print papers. Glue a box to each square.

Cut a bow shape, punch a 3/4-inch circle and cut a strip for ribbon from light blue, light yellow, light green and medium green card stock. Add blue ink to the edges of each piece the same as before. Glue the bows and ribbon strips to the gifts.

Use a computer and printer to print "celebrate," "wish," "holidays" and "merry" on white card stock. Cut out each label and attach each to a bow with a paper fastener.

Glue a photo to each gift. ❊

Creative Christmas Cards

Send loved ones special holiday wishes with these handcrafted greetings.

Ornament Card Will Decorate December

From Nina Guitierrez of Waukesha, Wisconsin, this stamped tree trim design (pictured above, at left) is certain to impress.

MATERIALS NEEDED:
Card stock—8-1/2-inch x 11-inch piece each of dark blue solid and brushed copper solid, 2-inch square of cream solid and two 2-inch squares each of dark green and red solid
Clear embossing ink stamp pad
Rubber stamps—antique background stamp, "Merry Christmas" stamp and ornament stamp (Nina used Stampin' Up stamps)
Blue embossing powder
Gold embossing powder
1-3/8-inch circle punch
1-1/4-inch circle punch
Double sided tape and pop dots
Heat gun
Thin copper cording
Scissors
Ruler
Pencil

FINISHED SIZE: Card is 4-1/4 inches wide x 5-1/2 inches high.

DIRECTIONS:
Cut dark blue solid card stock piece in half crosswise to make two 5-1/2-inch x 8-1/2-inch pieces. Fold one piece in half crosswise to make a 4-1/4-inch x 5-1/2-inch card.

Refer to card at left in photo above as a guide while stamping and assembling card.

Cut a 4-inch x 5-1/4-inch piece of copper solid card stock and tape it centered on front of folded card.

Cut a 3-3/4-inch x 5-inch piece of dark blue solid card stock. Stamp front of piece using clear embossing ink stamp pad and antique background stamp. When dry, center and tape stamped piece right side up to copper piece.

Stamp one square each of cream, dark green and red solid card stock with clear embossing ink stamp pad and a different ornament stamp. While ink is still wet, sprinkle each with gold embossing powder. Tap off excess powder. Use heat gun to melt powder on each. Let dry.

Use 1-1/4-inch circle punch to cut a circle from each embossed square. Then use 1-3/8-inch circle punch to cut a circle of copper, dark green and red card stock. Tape embossed cream circle right side up to center of copper circle. Tape remaining ornaments to matching larger circles.

Cut three 1-1/4-inch x 1/2-inch pieces of copper card stock. Tape one to the back of each ornament for top.

Cut three 1-inch lengths of copper cording. Fold each in half to make a loop. Tape the ends of each to the back of one ornament top for hanging loops.

Place card right side up on a flat surface with the fold at the left. Using pop dots, adhere the three ornaments to the front of the card.

Cut four 4-inch lengths of copper cording. Thread one piece through the loop on the top of each ornament. Tape ends together at the top of the card. Trim excess. Tie remaining piece in a bow on the top of center ornament.

Cut a 3-3/4-inch x 1-1/4-inch piece of copper card stock. Tape piece to top of card, leaving a narrow border of blue card stock showing at the top and covering the ends of the copper cording.

Cut a 3-5/8-inch x 1-1/8-inch piece of dark blue card stock. Tape piece centered on top of the copper piece.

Cut a 3-1/2-inch x 1-inch piece of copper card stock. Stamp front of piece using "Merry Christmas" stamp and clear stamp pad. While still wet, sprinkle stamped area with blue embossing powder. Tap off excess powder. Use heat gun to melt embossing powder. Let dry.

Tape stamped copper piece centered right side up to dark blue piece. ❀

Candy Card Makes The Season Sweet

This peppermint project (pictured above left, at center) by Tammy LeBlanc of Geismar, Louisiana goes together lickety-split.

MATERIALS NEEDED:
Card stock—9-1/2-inch x 6-7/8-inch piece of green solid, 3-3/4-inch x 6-inch piece of green-red-and-white stripe and 3-3/8-inch x 5-5/8-inch piece each of dark green solid, white solid and red solid
Scissors
Paper glue
Black fine-line marker
White gel pen
Red raffia

FINISHED SIZE: Card measures about 4-3/4 inches wide x 6-7/8 inches high.

DIRECTIONS:
Fold large green solid card stock piece in half crosswise to make a 4-3/4-inch-wide x 6-7/8-inch-high card.

Glue green-red-and-white stripe card stock piece to center front of card.

Glue dark green solid piece to center of stripe piece.

Cut a 5-1/4-inch-high candy cane shape from white card stock, trace shape onto red card stock and cut out. Cut red candy cane into pieces for stripes. Glue stripes to front of white candy cane. Glue candy cane to front of card.

Use marker to outline candy cane with long dashed lines and use gel pen to highlight outer edge of candy cane.

Tie raffia in a small bow. Glue bow to candy cane. ❀

Holly Leaf Card Is Berry Merry

Tammy LeBlanc of Geismar, Louisiana "grew" a greenery greeting (pictured at right in photo at left) that flourishes with fun.

MATERIALS NEEDED:
Pencil
Card stock—5-3/4-inch x 9-inch piece of red solid, 3-1/2-inch x 4-3/4-inch piece of off-white solid, 3-inch x 4-inch piece of green solid and 1/2-inch x 2-7/8-inch piece of tan solid
Three 1/2-inch red four-hole buttons
12-inch length of 3/8-inch-wide sheer tan ribbon
Craft or X-acto knife
Paper glue
Black and white gel pens
Ruler
Scissors

FINISHED SIZE: Holly card is 4-1/2 inches wide x 5-3/4 inches high.

DIRECTIONS:
Fold red card stock piece in half crosswise to make a 4-1/2-inch-wide x 5-3/4-inch-high card. Center and glue off-white card stock piece to the front of the card.

Place the opened card right side up on a hard, protected surface. Referring to photo for position, use craft or X-acto knife to cut a 3/8-inch-long slit through the front of the red card stock along opposite edges of the off-white piece about 1/8 inch from the top.

Working from the inside of the card, insert an end of the tan ribbon through each slit. Pull the ribbon ends to the left-hand side of the card and tie the ends in a double knot. Trim ribbon ends as shown in photo.

Draw three holly leaves on green card stock with pencil. Cut out each.

Use black gel pen to outline each holly leaf and to add center vein to each as shown in the photo.

Use white gel pen to add highlights to each holly leaf.

Apply a bead of glue down the center back of each holly leaf. Glue the holly leaves to the off-white area of the card. Glue the buttons to the ends of the holly leaves. Let dry.

Use black gel pen to write "Happy Holidays!" on tan card stock piece. Glue tan piece centered along bottom of off-white card stock piece. Let dry. ❀

World Cookie Exchange

This Christmas, why not give your holiday baking international flair? Discover new taste delights with these traditional cookies from—and inspired by—countries of the world.

England
Merry Christmas

🎄 English Tea Cakes

~Beverly Christian, Fort Worth, Texas

    2 cups butter, softened
    1 cup sugar
    2 teaspoons vanilla extract
    4 cups all-purpose flour
    60 walnut *or* pecan halves, toasted
Red colored sugar, optional

1. In a large mixing bowl, cream butter and sugar. Beat in vanilla. Gradually add flour. Drop by heaping tablespoonfuls into greased miniature muffin cups; flatten slightly. Press a walnut half into the center of each. Sprinkle with colored sugar if desired.

2. Bake at 350° for 10-12 minutes or until edges are lightly browned. Cool for 2 minutes before removing from pans to wire racks. **Yield:** 5 dozen.

English Tradition
Revelers pull Christmas crackers, colorful paper tubes that make a cracking sound and release goodies or gifts when pulled open.

Austria
Fröhliche Weihnachten

🎄 Sacher Torte Cookies

~Audrey Thibodeau, Fountain Hills, Arizona

    1 cup butter, softened
    1 package (3.9 ounces) instant chocolate pudding mix
    1 egg
    2 cups all-purpose flour
    1/4 cup sugar
    1/2 cup apricot, raspberry *or* strawberry preserves
GLAZE:
    1/3 cup semisweet chocolate chips
    1 tablespoon butter

1. In a large mixing bowl, cream butter and pudding mix. Beat in egg. Stir in flour until thoroughly combined. Shape dough into 1-1/4-in. balls; roll in sugar. Place 2 in. apart on ungreased baking sheets. Using the end of a wooden spoon handle, make an indentation in the center of each ball.

2. Bake at 325° for 15-18 minutes or until set. Cool for 2 minutes, remove to wire racks. Fill centers with preserves.

3. For glaze, in a small microwave-safe bowl, melt chocolate chips and butter. Cool slightly; stir until smooth. Drizzle over cookies. Cool completely. **Yield:** about 2-1/2 dozen.

Austrian Tradition
Carolers and musicians perform in church towers and village squares to "summon" churchgoers to worship services on Christmas Eve.

Sweden

🎄 Swedish Spice Cutouts

~Lilly Decker, Clancy, Montana

1-1/2 cups butter, softened
1-3/4 cups packed dark brown sugar
   1 egg
  2/3 cup dark corn syrup
  1/4 cup molasses
4-1/2 cups all-purpose flour
1-1/4 teaspoons ground cinnamon
   1 teaspoon baking soda
  3/4 teaspoon ground cloves
Slivered almonds, optional
Frosting of your choice, optional

1. In a large mixing bowl, cream butter and brown sugar. Beat in egg, corn syrup and molasses. Combine the flour, cinnamon, baking soda and cloves; gradually add to creamed mixture. Cover and refrigerate for 4 hours or until easy to handle.

2. On a lightly floured surface, roll dough to 1/8-in. thickness. Cut with floured 2-1/2-in. cookie cutters. Place 1 in. apart on ungreased baking sheets. Top with almonds if desired or leave plain. Bake at 375° for 8-10 minutes or until edges are lightly browned. Remove to wire racks to cool. Frost plain cookies if desired. **Yield:** about 10 dozen.

Swedish Tradition

A julbock, a straw goat bound with red ribbon that symbolizes rejuvenation and fertility, is placed underneath the Christmas tree.

France

🎄 Coconut Macaroons

~Naomi Vining, Springdale, Arkansas

  1/2 cup egg whites (about 4)
  1/4 teaspoon salt
1-1/4 cups sugar
  1/2 teaspoon vanilla extract
   3 cups flaked coconut
  30 red *or* green candied cherries, halved, optional

1. In a mixing bowl, beat egg whites and salt until soft peaks form. Gradually add sugar, beating until stiff peaks form, about 6 minutes. Beat in vanilla. Fold in coconut.

2. Drop by rounded teaspoonfuls 2 in. apart onto lightly greased baking sheets. Top each with a candied cherry half if desired. Bake at 325° for 20 minutes or until firm to the touch. Remove to wire racks to cool. **Yield:** 5 dozen.

French Tradition

Families gather together after Midnight Mass on Christmas Eve to share le réveillon, an extravagant feast that features a yule log-shaped cake.

Greece

▲ Greek Holiday Cookies

~Nicole Moskou, New York, New York

1-1/2 cups butter, softened
1-1/4 cups sugar
    4 eggs
    2 tablespoons orange juice
    3 teaspoons vanilla extract
5-1/4 cups all-purpose flour
1-1/2 teaspoons baking powder
    3/4 teaspoon baking soda

1. In a large mixing bowl, cream butter and sugar. Add 2 eggs; beat well. Beat in orange juice and vanilla. Combine the flour, baking powder and baking soda; gradually add to creamed mixture. Cover and refrigerate for 1 hour or until easy to handle.

2. Roll dough into 1-1/4-in. balls. Shape each into a 6-in. rope; fold in half and twist twice. Place 2 in. apart on ungreased baking sheets.

3. In a small bowl, beat the remaining eggs; brush over dough. Bake at 350° for 7-12 minutes or until edges are golden brown. Remove to wire racks. **Yield:** about 6-1/2 dozen.

Greek Tradition

Families light a fire in the fireplace to ward off kallikantzari, legendary goblins that sneak down chimneys at Christmas to cause mischief.

Germany

▲ Chocolate-Dipped Spritz

~Nancy Ross, Alvordton, Ohio

    1 cup butter, softened
  3/4 cup sugar
    1 egg
    1 teaspoon vanilla extract
2-1/4 cups all-purpose flour
  1/2 teaspoon salt
  1/4 teaspoon baking powder
 11 ounces dark, white *or* milk chocolate candy coating
Crushed peppermint candies, optional

1. In a large mixing bowl, cream butter and sugar. Beat in egg and vanilla. Combine the flour, salt and baking powder; gradually add to creamed mixture.

2. Using a cookie press fitted with disk, press dough 2 in. apart onto ungreased baking sheets. Bake at 375° for 7-9 minutes or until set (do not brown). Remove to wire racks to cool.

3. In a microwave-safe bowl, melt candy coating; dip each cookie halfway. Sprinkle with crushed candies if desired. Place on waxed paper until set. **Yield:** about 6 dozen.

German Tradition

Parents decorate the family Christmas tree in private on Christmas Eve before presenting the trimmed tree and gifts to their children.

🎄 Italian Sprinkle Cookies

~Gloria Cracchiolo, Newburgh, New York

6 eggs
5 cups all-purpose flour
2 cups confectioners' sugar
2 tablespoons plus 1-1/2 teaspoons baking powder
1 cup shortening
3 teaspoons almond extract
1-1/2 teaspoons lemon extract
GLAZE:
3-3/4 cups confectioners' sugar
1/2 cup warm milk
1 teaspoon almond extract
1 teaspoon vanilla extract
Colored sprinkles

1. Using a heavy-duty mixer, beat eggs on high speed until light and foamy, about 5 minutes; set aside. In a large mixing bowl, combine the flour, confectioners' sugar and baking powder; on low speed, gradually beat in shortening and extracts until mixture resembles fine crumbs. Gradually add beaten eggs (dough will be stiff).

2. Roll dough into 1-in. balls. Place 2 in. apart on ungreased baking sheets. Bake at 350° for 12-14 minutes (tops of the cookies will not brown, but bottoms should brown slightly).

3. Meanwhile, in a small bowl, combine the confectioners' sugar, milk and extracts until smooth. As soon as cookies are removed from the oven, quickly dip two or three at a time into glaze. Remove with a slotted spoon or tongs; place on wire racks to drain. Immediately top with sprinkles. Let dry for 24 hours before storing in airtight containers. **Yield:** about 7 dozen.

Italian Tradition

The legendary La Befana, a kind female witch with a broom, brings Italian children gifts on Epiphany, the last day of the Christmas season.

— Host a World Cookie Exchange —

🎄 In the invitations for your World Cookie Exchange, ask guests to bring cookies that represent their heritage…or any favorite ethnic cookies.

🎄 Request that guests bring one dozen cookies for each person at the event and to pack each dozen in a separate, inexpensive container for guests to take home. Ask them to bring an additional dozen for munching at the party. (Don't make the guest list too long!)

🎄 Note in the invitation that guests should give the "password" before entering the party—a cheery "Merry Christmas" in the language that corresponds to their cookies!

🎄 Contact guests before the party to find out what recipe they plan to make. That way, you can avoid having duplicate cookies.

🎄 Give your home international flair with decorations such as globe balloons, small national flags and a world map for a table runner. Or, share your own heritage by using decorations that reflect your family's country of origin.

'Merry Christmas' Around the World

Brazil
Feliz natal

China
Sheng dan kuai le

Croatia
Sretan Bozic

Denmark
Glædelig Jul

Finland
Hyvää Joulua

Hawaii
Mele Kalikimaka

Hungary
Boldog Karácsonyi Ünnepeket

Lithuania
Linksmu Kaledu

Mexico
Feliz Navidad

The Netherlands
Gelukkig Kerstfeest

Norway
God Jul

Poland
Wesolych swiat

Portugal
Feliz natal

Russia
Vesëlogo Rozhdestva

Spain
Feliz Navidad

Turkey
Neseli Noel

Our CHRISTMAS ANGELS

SANTA'S LITTLE HELPER. With his twinkling eyes and rosy cheeks, Paul Lloyd could be the spitting image of a young Kris Kringle. He's certainly a jolly little elf in the eyes of Grandma Polly Lloyd, Burlington, Wisconsin.

O CHRISTMAS TREE! At 7 months old, Tate Martin isn't too young to appreciate a holiday evergreen. "We have photographs of his mother, at age 2 months, sitting in the same little rocking chair," adds Grandma Charlotte McClain from O'Fallon, Missouri.

THE BEST THINGS come in small packages—as proven by Ella Roaldson perched inside a gift-wrapped box. "No grandmother could ask for a better present," writes Grandma Lana Jones of Glasgow, Montana.

"MMMM!" The Christmas cookies Mom Lara made to give the neighbors proved irresistible to Hannah Morris. "Hannah loves to help with holiday baking," shares Grandma Joan Dinsmore, Oakville, Ontario.

LITTLE NATIVITY. Joan White of Bremerton, Washington considers this photo of four of her grandchildren, Stephanie, Kevin, Katie and Sarah, to be a special gift. "It always reminds me of the reason for the Christmas season," she writes.

BEAR-Y CHRISTMAS. Is it time for the holiday parade? Or maybe a party? Either way, 9-month-old Trevor King and his bears are all dressed and ready to go. Great-aunt Karen Van Beek sends this photo from Pipestone, Minnesota.

May the magic of Christmas fill you and yours with wonder and joy this holiday season and throughout the New Year.

 # Index

Food

Crafts

Share Your Holiday Joy!

DO YOU celebrate Christmas in a special way? If so, we'd like to know! We're already gathering material for our next *Country Woman Christmas* book. And we need your help!

Do you have a nostalgic holiday-related story to share? Perhaps you have penned a Christmas poem...or a heartwarming fiction story?

Does your family carry on a favorite holiday tradition? Or do you deck your halls in some festive way? Maybe you know of a Christmas-loving country woman others might like to meet?

We're looking for *original* Christmas quilt patterns and craft projects, plus homemade Nativities, gingerbread houses, etc. Don't forget to include your best recipes for holiday-favorite main-dish meats, home-baked cookies, candies, breads, etc.!

Send your ideas and photos to "CW Christmas Book," 5925 Country Lane, Greendale WI 53129. (Enclose a self-addressed stamped envelope if you'd like materials returned.) ▲